McGarry Library
Saint Francis College

180 REMSEN STREET
BROOKLYN, N. Y.

A Garland Series

British Philosophers and Theologians of the 17th & 18th Centuries

A Collection of 101 Volumes

Edited by
René Wellek

John Bramhall

A
DEFENCE
OF
TRUE LIBERTY
1655

Garland Publishing, Inc., New York & London

1977

Bibliographical note:

this facsimile has been made from a copy in the
Bodleian Library of Oxford University
(8° .G.60.ART)

Library of Congress Cataloging in Publication Data

Bramhall, John, Abp. of Armagh, 1594-1663.
  A defence of true liberty, 1655.

  (British philosophers and theologians of the 17th and
18th centuries)
  Reprint of the 1655 ed. printed for J. Crook, London.
  1. Hobbes, Thomas, 1588-1679. Of liberty and
necessity. 2. Free will and determinism. 3. Necessity
(Philosophy) I. Title. II. Series.
B1234.B7 1977   123   75-11200
ISBN 0-8240-1756-0

Printed in the United States of America

A DEFENCE OF TRUE LIBERTY FROM ANTECEDENT AND *Extrinsecall Necessity*,

Being an answer to a late Book of *Mr. Thomas Hobbs* of *Malmsbury*, intituled, *A Treatise of Liberty and Necessity*.

Written by the Right Reverend *John Bramhall* D. D. and Lord Bishop of *Derry*.

LONDON,
Printed for *John Crook*, and are to be sold at his Shop at the sign of the Ship in St. *Pauls* Church-yard, 1655.

To the Right Honourable the Marquis of New-castle, &c.

S IR,
If I pretended to compose a complete treatise upon this subject, I should not refuse those large recruites of reasons and authorities, which offer themselves to serve in this cause, for God and man, Religion and Policy, Church & Common-wealth, against the blasphemous, desperate, and destructive opinion of
fatall

fatall destiny. But as mine aim, in the first discourse, was onely to press home those things in writing, which had been agitated between us by word of mouth, (a course much to be preferred before verball conferences, as being freer from passions and tergiversations, less subject to mistakes and misrelations, wherein paralogismes are more quickly detected, impertinencies discovered, & confusion avoided.) So my present intention is onely to vindicate that discourse, and together with it, those lights of the Schooles, who were never sleighted, but where they

they were not understood. How far I have performed it, I leave to the judicious and unpartiall Reader, resting for mine own part well contented with this, that I have satisfied my self.

*Your Lorships most obliged
to love and serve you*

I. D.

TO THE READER.

CHristian Reader, this ensuing treatise was neither penned nor intended for the Press, but privately undertaken, that by the ventilation of the question, truth might be cleared from mistakes. The same was Mr. Hobbs his desire at that time, as appeareth by four passages in his Book, wherein he requesteth and beseecheth, P. 18. that it may be kept private. But either through forget- 26.35. fulness or change of judgment, he hath now caused, or & 30. permitted it to be printed in England, without either adjoining my first discourse, to which he wrote that answer, or so much as mentioning this Reply, which he hath had in his hands now these eight years. So wide is the date of his letter, in the year 1652. from the truth, and his manner of dealing with me in this particular from ingenuity, (if the edition were with his own consent.) Howsoever here is all that passed between us upon this subject, without any addition, or the least variation from the originall.

Concerning the nameless Authour of the preface, who takes upon him to hang out an Ivy bush before this rare piece of sublimated Stoacisme, to invite passengers to purchase it, As I know not who he is, so I do not much heed it, nor regard, either his ignorant censures, or hyperbolicall expressions. The Church of England is as much above his detraction, as he is beneath this question. Let him lick up the spittle of Dionysius by himself, as his servile flatterers did, and protest, that it is more sweet than Nectar; we envie him not, much good may it do him. His very frontispiece is a sufficient confutation of his whole preface, wherein he tells the world as falsly

and

and ignorantly, as confidently, that all controversy, concerning Predestination, Election, Free-will, Grace, Merits, Reprobation, &c. is fully decided and cleared. Thus he accustometh his pen to run over, beyond all limits of truth and discretion, to let us see that his knowledge in Theologicall Controversies is none at all, and into what miserable times we are fallen, when blind men will be the onely judges of colours. Quid tanto dignum feret hic promissor hiatu?

    There is yet one thing more, whereof I desire to advertise the Reader. Whereas Mr. Hobbs mentions my objections to his Book De Cive; It is true, that ten yeares since I gave him about 60. exceptions, the one half of them Politicall, the other half Theologicall, to that Book, and every exception justified by a number of reasons, to which he never yet vouchsafed any answer. Nor do I now desire it, for since that, he hath published his Leviathan: Monstrum horrendum, informe, ingens, cui lumen ademptum, which affords much more matter of exception. And I am informed that there are already two, the one of our own Church, the other a stranger, who have shaken in pieces the whole Fabrick of his City, that was but builded in the air, and resolved that huge mass of his seeming Leviathan into a new nothing, and that their labours will speedily be published. But if this information should not prove true, I will not grudge upon his desire, God willing, to demonstrate, that his principles are pernicious, both to Piety and Policy, and destructive to all relations of mankind, between Prince and Subject, Father and Child, Master and Servant, Husband and Wife; And that they, who maintain them obstinately, are fitter to live in hollow-trees among wild beasts, than in any Christian or Politicall Society, so God bless us.

P. 1.

A

(1)

A VINDICATION OF TRUE LIBERTY FROM
Antecedent and Extrinsecal Necessity.

J. D.

Ither I am free to write Numb.1. this discourse for Liberty against Necessity, or I am not free. If I have obteined the cause, and ought not to suffer for the truth. If I be not free, yet I ought not to be blamed, since I do it not out of any voluntary election, but out of an inevitable necessity.

B *T. H.*

T. H.

*R*Ight Honourable, I had once resolved to answer J. D's. objections to my Book De Cive in the first place, as that which concerns me most, and afterwards to examine this discourse of Liberty and Necessity, which (because I never had uttered my opinion of it) concerned me the less. But seeing it was both your Lordships, and J. D's. desire, that I should begin with the latter, I was contented so to do. And here I present and submit it to your Lordships judgement.

J. D.

THe first day that I did read over *T. H.* his defence of the necessity of all things, was *April* 20. 1646. which proceeded not out of any disrespect to him; for if all his discourses had been Geometrical demonstrations, able not onely to perswade, but also to compell assent, all had been one to me, first my journey, and afterwards some other trifles (which we call business) having diverted me untill then. And then my occasions permitting me, and an advertisement from a friend awakening me, I set my self to a serious examination of it. We commonly see those who delight in Paradoxes, if they have line enough, confute themselves, and their speculatives, and their practicks familiarly enterferre one with another. The very first words of *T. H.* his defence trip up the heels of his whole cause; *I had once resol-*

resolved; To resolve præsupposeth deliberation, but what deliberation can there be of that which is inevitably determined by causes, without our selves, before we do deliberate? can a condemned man deliberate whether he should be executed, or not? It is even to as much purpose, as for a man to consult and ponder with himself whether he should draw in his Breath, or whether he should increase in stature. Secondly, *to resolve* implies a mans dominion over his own actions, and his actuall determination of himself; but he who holds an absolute necessity of all things, hath quitted this dominion over himself, and (which is worse) hath quitted it to the second extrinsecal causes, in which he makes all his actions to be determined; one may as well call again Yesterday, as *resolve*, or newly determine that which is determined to his hand already. I have perused this treatise, weighed *T. H.* his answers, considered his reasons, and conclude that he hath missed and misled the question, that the answers are evasions, that his Arguments are parologisms, that the opinion of absolute and universall necessity is but a result of some groundless and ill chosen principles, and that the defect is not in himself, but that his cause will admit no better defence; and therefore by his favour I am resolved to adhere to my first opinion, perhaps

haps another man reading this discourse with other eyes, judgeth it to be pertinent and well founded; How comes this to pass? the treatise is the same, the exteriour causes are the same, yet the resolution is contrary. Do the second causes play fast and loose? do they necessitate me to condemn, and necessitate him to maintain? what is it then? the difference must be in our selves, either in our intellectuals, because the one sees clearer then the other, or in our affections, which betray our understandings, and produce an implicite adhærence in the one more than in the other. Howsoever it be, the difference is in our selves. The outward causes alone do not chain me to the one resolution, nor him to the other resolution. But *T. H.* may say, that our severall and respective deliberations and affections, are in part the causes of our contrary resolutions, and do concur with the outward causes, to make up one totall and adæquate cause, to the necessary production of this effect. If it be so, he hath spun a fair thred, to make all this stir for such a necessity as no man ever denied or doubted of; when all the causes have actually determined themselves, then the effect is in being; for though there be a priority in nature between the cause and the effect, yet they are together in time. And the old rule is, *whatsoever is, when it is, is necessarily so*

as

as it is. This is no absolute necessity, but onely upon supposition, that a man hath determined his own liberty. When we question whether all occurrences be necessary, we do not question, whether they be necessary when they are, nor whether they be necessary *in sensu composito*, after we have resolved, and finally determined what to do, but whether they were necessary before they were determined by our selves, by or in the præcedent causes before our selves, or in the exterior causes without our selves. It is not inconsistent with true liberty to determine it self, but it is inconsistent with true liberty to be determined by another without it self.

T. H. saith further, *that upon your Lordships desire and mine, he was contented to begin with this discourse of liberty and necessity,* that is, to change his former resolution. If the chain of necessity be no stronger, but that it may be snapped so easily in sunder, if his will was no otherwise determiued from without himself, but onely by the signification of your Lordships desire, and my modest intreaty, then we may safely conclude, that humane affairs are not alwaies governed by absolute necessity, that a man is Lord of his own actions, if not in chief, yet in mean, subordinate to the Lord Paramount of Heaven and Earth, and that all things are

not

not so absolutely determined in the outward and precedent causes, but that fair intreaties, and morall perswasions may work upon a good nature so far, as to prevent that which otherwise had been, and to produce that which otherwise had not been. He that can reconcile this with an Antecedent Necessity of all things, and a Physicall or naturall determination of all causes, shall be great *Apollo* to me.

Whereas *T. H.* saith that he had never uttered his opinion of this question, I suppose he intends in writing; my conversation with him hath not been frequent, yet I remember well, that when this question was agitated between us two in your Lordships Chamber by your command, he did then declare himself in words, both for the absolute necessity of all events, and for the ground of this necessity, the Flux or concatenation of the second causes.

T. H.

Numb. 2. **A**Nd *first I assure your Lordship, I find in it no new Argument, neither from Scripture nor from reason, that I have not often heard before, which is as much as to say, that I am not surprised.*

J. D.

THough I be so unhappy, that I can present no novelty to *T. H.* yet I have this comfort, that if he be not surprised, then in reason I may expect a more mature answer from him, and where he failes,

I

I may ascribe it to the weakness of his cause, not to want of preparation. But in this case I like *Epictetus* his Counsell well, that the Sheep should not brag how much they have eaten, or what an excellent pasture they do go in, but shew it in their Lamb and Wool. Apposite answers and downright Arguments advantage a cause. To tell what we have heard or seen is to no purpose, when a respondent leaves many things untouched, as if they were too hot for his Fingers, and declines the weight of other things, and alters the true state of the question, it is a shrewd sign either that he hath not weighed all things maturely, or else that he maintains a desperate cause.

T. H.

Numb. 3.

The Præface is an handsome one, but it appears even in that, that he hath mistaken the question; for whereas he saies thus, If I be free to write this discourse, I have obteined the cause, I deny that to be true, for 'tis not enough to his freedom of writing, that he had not written it, unless he would himself; if he will obtein the cause, he must prove that before he writ it, it was not necessary he should write it afterward. It may be he thinks it all one to say I was free to write it, and it was not necessary I should write it. But I think otherwise ; for he is free to do a thing, that may do it if he have the will to do it, and

may

may forbear if he have the will to forbear. And yet if there be a necessity that he shall have the will to do it, the action is necessarily to follow. And if there be a necessity, that he shall have the will to forbear, the forbearing also will be necessary. The question therefore is not, whether a man be a free agent, that is to say, whether he can write or forbear, speak or be silent, according to his will, but whether the will to write, and the will to forbear, come upon him according to his will, or according to any thing else in his own power. I acknowledge this liberty, that I can do if I will, but to say I can will if I will, I take it to be an absurd speech. Wherefore I cannot grant him the cause upon this Preface.

J. D.

TAcitus speaks of a close kind of adversaries, which evermore begin with a mans praise. The Crisis or the Catastrophe of their discourse is when they come to their, *but*, As he is a good natured man, *but* he hath *a* naughty quality; or he is a wise man, *but* he hath committed one of the greatest follies, So here the *Preface* is an handsome one, but it appears even in this, that he hath mistaken the question. This is to give an Inch, that one may take away an Ell without suspicion, to praise the handsomness of the Porch, that he may gain credit to the vilifying of the House. Whether of us hath mistaken the que-

queſtion, I refer to the judicious Reader. Thus much I will maintain, that, that is no true neceſſity, which he calls neceſſity, nor that liberty which he calls liberty, nor that the queſtion which he makes the queſtion.

Firſt for liberty, that which he calls liberty is no true liberty. 1.

For the clearing whereof it behooveth us to know the difference between theſe three, *Neceſſity*, *Spontaneity*, and *Liberty*.

Neceſſity and Spontaneity may ſometimes meet together, ſo may ſpontaneity and liberty, but reall neceſſity and true liberty can never meet together, ſomethings are neceſſary and not voluntary or ſpontaneous, ſomethings are both neceſſary and voluntary, ſomethings are voluntary and not free, ſomethings are both voluntary & free; But thoſe things which are truly neceſſary can never be free, and thoſe things which are truly free can never be neceſſary. Neceſſity conſiſts in an Antecedent determination to one, Spontaneity conſiſts in a conformity of the Appetite, either intellectual or ſenſitive to the object; True liberty conſiſts in the elective power of the rational will; That which is determined without my concurrence, may nevertheleſs agree well enough with my fancy or deſires, and obtein my ſubſequent conſent; But that which is determined without my concurrence or conſent, cannot be the object of mine election. I may like that which is inevitably impoſed upon me

by

by another, but if it be inevitably imposed upon me by extrinsecall causes, it is both folly for me to deliberate, and impossible for me to choose, whether I shall undergo it or not. Reason is the root, the fountain, the originall of true liberty, which judgeth and represententh to the will, whether this or that be convenient, whether this or that be more convenient. Judge then what a pretty kind of liberty it is which is maintained by *T. H.* such a liberty as is in little Children before they have the use of reason, before they can consult or deliberate of any thing. Is not this a Childish liberty? and such a liberty as is in brute Beasts, as Bees and Spiders, which do not learn their faculties as we do our trades, by experience and consideration; This is a brutish liberty, such a liberty as a Bird hath to flie, when her wings are clipped, or to use his own comparison, such a liberty as a lame man who hath lost the use of his lims hath to walk; Is not this a ridiculous liberty? Lastly (which is worse then all these) such a *liberty as a River hath to descend down the Channell*; what will he ascribe liberty to inanimate Creatures also, which have neither reason, nor spontaneity, nor so much as sensitive appetite? Such is *T. H.* his liberty.

His necessity is just such another, a necessity upon supposition, arising from the concourse

concourse of all the causes, including the last dictate of the understanding in reasonable creatures. The adæquate cause and the effect are together in time, and when all the concurrent causes are determined, the effect is determined also, and is become so necessary, that it is actually in being; But there is a great difference between determining, and being determined; if all the collaterall causes concurring to the production of an effect, were antecedently determined, what they must of necessity produce, and when they must produce it, then there is no doubt but the effect is necessary. But if these causes did operate freely, or contingently, if they might have suspended or denied their concurrence, or have concurred after another manner, then the effect was not truly and Antecedently necessary but either free or contingent. This will be yet clearer by considering his own instance of *casting Ambs-Ace*, though it partake more of contingency then of freedom. Supposing the positure of the parties hand who did throw the Dice, supposing the figure of the Table and of the Dice themselves, supposing the measure of force applied, and supposing all other things which did concur to the production of that cast, to be the very same they were, there is no doubt but in this case the cast is necessary. But still this is but a necessity

cessity of supposition; for if all these concurrent causes or some of them were contingent or free, then the cast was not absolutely necessary. To begin with the Caster, He might have denied his concurrence and not have cast at all; He might have suspended his concurrence, and not have cast so soon; He might have doubled or diminished his force in casting, if it had pleased him; He might have thrown the dice into the other table. In all these cases what becomes of his *ambs-ace*? The like uncertainties offer themselves for the maker of the tables, and for the maker of the dice, and for the keeper of the tables, and for the kind of wood, and I know not how many other circumstances. In such a mass of contingencies, it is impossible that the effect should be antecedently necessary. *T. H.* appeales to every mans experience. I am contented. Let every one reflect upon himself, and he shall find no convincing, much less constreining reason, to necessitate him to any one of these particular acts more than another, but onely his own will or arbitrary determination. So *T. H.* his necessity is no absolute, no antecedent, extrinsecall necessity, but meerly a necessity upon supposition.

3   Thirdly, that which *T. H.* makes the question, is not the question. The question is not, saith he, *Whether a man may write if he will, and forbear if he will, but whether*

ther the will to write or the will to forbear come upon him according to his will, or according to any thing els in his own power. Here is a distinction without a difference. If his will do not come upon him according to his will, then he is not a free, nor yet so much as a voluntary agent, which is *T. H.* his liberty. Certainly all the freedom of the agent is from the freedom of the will. If the will have no power over it self, the agent is no more free than a staff in a mans hand. Secondly, he makes but an empty shew of a power in the will, either to write or not to write. If it be precisely and inevitably determined in all occurrences whatsoever, what a man shall will, and what he shall not will, what he shall write, and what he shall not write, to what purpose is this power? God and Nature never made any thing in vain, but vain and frustraneous is that power which never was and never shall be deduced into Act. Either the agent is determined before he acteth, what he shall will, and what he shall not will, what he shall act, and what he shall not act, and then he is no more free to act than he is to will. Or els he is not determined, and then there is no necessity. No effect can exceed the vertue of its cause; if the action be free to write or to forbear, the power or faculty to will, or nill, must of necessity be more free. *Quod efficit tale illud magis est tale.*

If the will be determined, the writing or not writing is likewife determined, and then he fhould not fay, *he may write or he may forbear*, but he muft write, or he muft forbear. Thirdly, this anfwer contradicts the fenfe of all the world, that the will of man is determined *without his will, or without any thing in his power*; Why do we ask men whether they will do fuch a thing or not? Why do we reprefent reafons to them? Why do we pray them? Why do we intreat them? Why do we blame them if their will come not upon them according to their will. *Wilt thou be made clean?* faid our Saviour to the *Paralitike* perfon, *John* 5. 6. to what purpofe if his will was extrinfecally determined? Chrift complains, *We have piped unto you, and ye have not danced*, Matth. 11. 17. How could they help it, if their wills were determined without their wills to forbear? And Matth. 23. 37. *I would have gathered your children together as the Hen gathereth her Chickens under her wings, but ye would not.* How eafily might they anfwer according to *T. H.* his doctrine, Alas blame not us, Our wills are not in our own power or difpofition, if they were, we would thankfully embrace fo great a favour.

De *lib. Au.* Moft truly faid St. Auftin, *Our will fhould*
l. 3. c. 30. *not be a will at all, if it were not in our power.* This is the belief of all mankind, which we have not learned from our Tutors

tors, but is imprinted in our hearts by nature; We need not turn over any obscure books to find out this truth. The Poets chant it in the Theaters, the Shepheards in the mountains, The Pastors teach it in their Churches, the Doctors in the Universities. The common people in the marketts, and all mankind in the whole world do assent unto it, except an handfull of men, who have poisoned their intellectualls with paradoxicall principles. Fourthly, this necessity which *T. H.* hath devised, which is grounded upon the necessitation of a mans will without his will, is the worst of all others, and is so far from lessening those difficulties and absurdities which flow from the fatall destiny of the *Stoicks*, that it increaseth them, and rendreth them unanswerable. No man blameth fire for burning whole Cities, No man taxeth poison for destroying men, but those persons who apply them to such wicked ends. If the will of man be not in his own disposition, he is no more a free agent than the fire or the poison. Three things are required to make an act or omission culpable; First, that it be in our power to perform it, or forbear it, Secondly, that we be obliged to perform it, or forbear it respectively. Thirdly, that we omit that which we ought to have done, or do that which we ought to have omitted. No man sins in doing those things
which

which he could not shun, or forbearing those things which never were in his power. *T. H.* may say, that besides the power, men have also an appetite to evill objects, which renders them culpable. It is true, but if this appetite be determined by anothers, not by themselves, Or if they have not the use of reason to curb or restrain their appetites, they sin no more than a stone descending downeward, according to its naturall appetite, or the brute beasts who commit voluntary errours in following their sensitive appetites, yet sin not.

The question then is not whether a man be necessitated to will or nill, yet free to act or forebear. But having the ambiguous acceptions of the word, free, the question is plainly this, whether all agents, and all events natural, civill, moral (for we speak not now of the conversion of a sinner, that concerns not this question,) be predetermined extrinsecally and inevitably without their own concurrence in the determination; so as all actions and events which either are or shall be, cannot but be, nor can be otherwise, after any other manner, or in any other place, time, number, measure, order, nor to any other end, than they are. And all this in respect of the supreme cause, or a concourse of extrinsecall causes determining them to one.

So my preface remaines yet unanswered.
Either

Either I was extrinsecally and inevitably predetermined to write this discourse, without any concurrence of mine in the determination, and without any power in me to change or oppose it, or I was not so predetermined; If I was, then I ought not to be blamed, for no man is justly blamed for doing that which never was in his power to shun. If I was not so predetermined, then mine actions and my will to act, are neither compelled nor necessitated by any extrinsecall causes, but I elect and choose, either to write or to forbear, according to mine own will, and by mine own power. And when I have resolved, and elected, it is but a necessity of supposition, which may and doth consist with true liberty, not a real anteeedent necessity. The two hornes of this Dilemma are so strait, that no mean can be given, nor room to pass between them. And the two consequences are so evident, that in stead of answering, he is forced to decline them.

J. D.

AND so to fall in hand with the question, without any further proems or prefaces. By liberty, I do understand neither a liberty from sin, nor a liberty from misery, nor a liberty from servitude, nor a liberty from violence, but I understand a liberty from necessity or rather from necessitation, that is, an universall immunity from all inevitability and determination to one, whether it be of the *exercise* only which the Schooles call a liberty of *contradiction*, and is found in God, and in the good and bad Angells, that is not a liber-

Numb. 4.

ty to do both good and evill, but a liberty to do or not to do this or that good, this or that evill respectively; or whether it be a liberty of *specification and exercise* also, which the Schooles call liberty of *contrariety*, and is found in men indowed with reason and understanding, that is a liberty to do and not to do, good and evill, this or that. Thus the coast being cleared, &c.

T. H.

IN the next place he maketh certain *distinctions of liberty*, and sayes, he meanes not liberty from sin, nor from servitude, nor from violence, but from necessity, necessitation, inevitability, and determination to one; It had been better to define liberty than thus to distinguish, for I understand never the more what he meanes by liberty. And though he sayes, he meanes liberty from necessitation, yet I understand not how such a liberty can be, and it is a taking of the question without proof, for what els is the question between us but whether such a liberty be possible or not. There are in the same place other distinctions, as a liberty of exercise only, which he calls a liberty of contradiction, (namely, of doing not good or evill simply, but of doing this or that good, or this or that evill respectively.) And a liberty of specification and exercise also, which he calls a liberty of contrariety, namely, a liberty not only to do or not do, good or evill, but also to do or not do, this or that good or evill. And with these distinctions he sayes, he cleares the coast, whereas in truth he darkeneth his meaning,

not

not onely with the Jargon of exercise onely, specification also, contradiction, contrariety, but also with pretending distinction where none is, for how is it possible for the liberty of doing or not doing, this or that good or evill, to consist (as he sayes it doth in God and Angells) without a liberty of doing or not doing good or evill.

J. D.

IT is a rule in art, that words which are homonymous, of various and ambiguous significations, ought ever in the first place to be distinguished. No men delight in confused generalities, but either Sophisters or Bunglers. *Vir dolosus versatur in generalibus*, deceitfull men do not love to descend to particulars; and when bad Archers shoot, the safest way is to run to the marke. Liberty is sometimes opposed to the slavery of sin and vitious habits, as Rom. 6. 22. *Now being made free from sin*. Sometimes to misery and oppression, Isay 58. 6. *To let the oppressed go free.* Sometimes to servitude, as Levit. 25. 10. *In the year of Jubilee ye shall proclaim liberty throughout the land.* Sometimes to violence, as Psal. 105. 20. *The prince of his people let him go free.* Yet none of all these are the liberty now in question, but a liberty from necessity, that is a determination to one, or rather from necessitation that is a necessity imposed by another, or an extrinsecall determination. These distinctions, do virtually imply a description of true liberty, which comes neerer the essence of it, then *T. H.* his roving definition as we shall see in due place. And though he say that *he understands never the more what I mean by liberty*, yet it is plain by his own ingenuous confession, both that he doth understand it, and that this is the very question where the water sticks between us, whether there be such a liberty free from all necessitation and extrinsecall determination to one. Which being but the stating of the question, he calls it amiss *the taking of the question*. It were too much weaknesse to beg this question, which is so copious and demonstrable. It is strange to see with what confidence now adayes particular men slight all the Schoolemen, and Philosophers, and Classick Authors of former ages, as if they were not worthy to unloose the shoe-strings of some moderne Author, or did sit in darknesse, and in the shadow of death, untill some third *Cato* dropped down from heaven, to whom all men must repaire, as to the Altar of *Promotheus*, to light their torches. I did never wonder to heare a raw Divine out of the Pulpit declare against Schoole Divinity to his equally ignorant Auditors; It is but as the Fox in the Fable, who having lost his own taile by a mischance, would have perswaded all his fellowes to cut off theirs, and throw them away as unprofitable burthens. But it troubles me to see a Scholar, one who hath been long admitted into the innermost closet of nature, and seene the hidden secrets of more subtil learning, so far to forget himself, as to stile Schoole-learning no better than a plain *Jargon*, that is a senselesse gibrish, or a fustian language, like the clattering noyse of Sabots, suppose they

did

did sometimes too much cut truth into shreds, or delight in abstruse expressions, yet certainly, this distinction of liberty, into liberty of *contrariety* and liberty of contradiction, or which is all one, of *exercise onely*, or *exercise and specification jointly*, which *T. H.* rejects with so much scorn, is so true, so necessary, so generally received, that there is scarce that writer of note, either Divine or Philosopher, who did ever treat upon this subject, but he useth it.

Good and evill are contraries, or opposite kinds of things, therefore to be able to choose both good and evill, is a liberty of contrariety or of specification; To choose this, and not to choose this, are contradictory, or which is all one, an exercise or suspension of power; Therefore to be able to do or forbear to do the same action, to choose or not choose the same object, without varying of the kind, is a liberty of contradiction, or of exercise onely. Now man is not onely able to do or forbear to do good onely, or evill onely, but he is able both to do and to forbear to do, both good and evill; so he hath not onely a liberty of the action, but also a liberty of contrary objects; not onely a liberty of exercise, but also of specification; not onely a liberty of contradiction, but also of contrariety. On the other side, God and the good Angels, can do or not do this or that good, but they cannot do and not do, both good and evill. So they have onely a liberty of exercise or contradiction, but not a liberty of specification or contrariety. It appears then plainly, that the liberty of man is more large in the

extension

extenſion of the object, which is both good and evill, then the liberty of God and the good Angels, whoſe object is onely good. But withall, the liberty of man comes ſhort in the intenſion of the power. Man is not ſo free in reſpect of good onely, as God, or the good Angels, becauſe (not to ſpeak of God whoſe liberty is quite of another nature) the underſtandings of the Angels are clearer, their power and domion over their actions is greater, they have no ſenſitive appetites to diſtract them, no Organs to be diſturbed; we ſee then this diſtinction is cleared from all darkneſs.

And where *T. H.* demands how it is poſſible for the liberty of doing, or not doing this or that good or evill, to conſiſt in God and Angels, without a liberty of doing or not doing good or evill. The anſwer is obvious and eaſy, *referendo ſingula ſingulis*, rendering every act to its right object reſpectively. God and good Angels have a power to do or not to do this or that good, bad Angels have a power to do or not to do this or that evill, ſo both joyntly conſidered, have power reſpectively to do good or evill. And yet according to the words of my diſcourſe, God, and good, and bad Angels being ſingly conſidered, have no power to do good or evill, that is, indifferently, as man hath.

J. D.

Numb.5. THus the coaſt being cleared, the next thing to be done, is to draw out our forces againſt the enemy; And becauſe they are divided into

two

two Squadrons, the one of Christians, the other of Heathen Philosophers, it will be best to dispose ours also into two Bodies, the former drawn from Scripture, the latter from Reason.

T. H.

THe next thing he doth after the clearing of the coast, is the dividing of his forces, as he calls them into two Squadrons, one of places of Scripture, the other of reasons, which Allegory he useth, I suppose because he adresseth the discourse to your Lordship, who is a Military Man. All that I have to say, touching this is, that I observe a great part of those his forces, do look and march another way, and some of them do fight among themselves.

J. D.

IF T. H. could divide my forces, and commit them together among themselves, it were his onely way to conquer them. But he will find that those imaginary contradictions, which he thinks he hath espied in my discourse, are but fancies, And my supposed impertinencies will prove his own reall mistakings.

J. D.
Proofs of liberty out of Scripture.

FIrst, whosoever have power of election have true liberty, for the proper act of liberty is election. A Spontaneity may consist with determination to one, as we see in Children, Fools, mad Men, bruit Beasts, whose fancies are determined to those things which they act spontaneously, as the Bees makes Hony, the

Numb. 1

Spiders

Spiders Webs. But none of these have a liberty of election, which is an act of judgement and understanding, and cannot possibly consist with a determination to one. He that is determined by something before himself or without himself, cannot be said to choose or elect, unless it be as the *Junior* of the Mess chooseth in *Cambridge*, whether he will have the least *Paul* or nothing. And scarcely so much.

But men have liberty of election. This is plain *Numb.* 30. 14. If a Wife make a vow its left to her Husbands choice, either to establish it or to make it void. And *Josh.* 24. 15. *Choose you this day whom ye will serve,* &c. *But I and my house will serve the Lord.* He makes his own choice, and leaves them to the liberty of of their election. And 2 *Sam.* 24. 12. *I offer thee three things, choose thee which of them I shall do.* If one of these three things was necessarily determined, and the other two impossible, how was it left to him to choose what should be done ? Therefore we have true liberty.

T. H.

And the first place of Scripture taken from Numb. 30. 14. *is one of them that look another way; The words are, If a Wife make a vow, it is left to her Husbands choice, either to establish it or make it void, for it prooves no more but that the Husband is a free or voluntary Agent, but not that his choice therein is not necessitated or not determined, to what he shall choose by præcedent necessary causes.*

J. D.

J. D.

MY first Argument from Scripture is thus *Arg.* 1. formed, Whosoever have a liberty or power of election, are not determined to one by præcedent necessary causes.

But Men have liberty of election.

The assumtion or *minor* proposition is prooved by three places of Scripture, *Numb.* 30.14. *Josh.* 24.15. 2 *Sam.* 24, 12. I need not insist upon these, because *T. H.* acknowledgeth, *that it is clearly prooved that there is election in Man.*

But he denieth the *major* Proposition, because (saith he) man *is necessitated or determined to what he shall choose* by præcedent necessary causes; I take away this answer three wayes.

First, by reason; election is evermore either of things possible, or at least of things conceived to be possible, That is efficacious election, when a man hopeth or thinketh of obteining the object. Whatsoever the will chooseth, it chooseth under the notion of good, either honest or delightfull or profitable, but there can be no reall goodness apprehended in that which is known to be impossible: It is true, there may be some wandring perdulous wishes of known impossibilities, as a man also hath committed an offence, may wish he had not committed it, But to choose effiaciously and impossibly, is as impossible as an impossibility it self. No man can think to obtein that which he knows impossible to be obteined, But he who

knows

knows that all things are antecedently determined by necessary causes, knows that it is impossible for any thing to be otherwise then it is; Therefore to ascribe unto him a power of election, to choose this or that indifferently, is to make the same thing to be determined to one, and to be not determined to one, which are contradictories. Again, whosoever hath an elective power or a liberty to choose, hath also a liberty or power to refuse, *Isa.*7.10. *Before the Child shall know to refuse the evill and choose the good.* He who chooseth this rather then that, refuseth that rather then this. As *Moses* choosing to suffer affliction with the people of God, did thereby refuse the pleasures of sin. *Heb.* 11. 24. But no man hath any power to refuse, that which is necessarily prædetermined to be, unless it be as the Fox refused the Grapes which were beyond his reach. When one thing of two or three is absolutely determined, the other are made thereby simply impossible.

2   Secondly, I proove it by instances, and by that universal notion, which the world hath of election; what is the difference between an elective and hereditary Kingdom? but that in an elective Kingdom they have power or liberty to choose this or that Man indifferently, But in an hæreditary Kingdom they have no such power nor liberty. Where the Law makes a certain Heir, there is a necessitation to one; where the Law doth not name a certain Heir, there is no necessitation to one, and there they have power or liberty to choose. An hæreditary

tary Prince may be as gratefull and acceptable to his subjects, and as willingly received by them (according to that liberty which is opposed to compulsion or violence) as he who is chosen, yet he is not therefore an elective Prince. In *Germany* all the Nobility and Commons may assent to the choise of the Emperour, or be well pleased with it when it is concluded, yet none of them elect or choose the Emperour, but onely those six Princes who have a consultative, deliberative, and determinative power in his Election. And if their votes or suffrages be equally divided, three to three, then the King of *Bohemia* hath the casting voice. So likewise in Corporations or Commonwealths, sometimes the people, sometimes the Common Councell, have power to name so many persons for such an office, and the Supreme Magistrate, or Senate, or lesser Councell respectively, to choose one of those. And all this is done with that caution and secrecy, by billetts or other means, that no man knowes which way any man gave his vote, or with whom to be offended. If it were necessarily and inevitably predetermined, that this individuall person and no other shall and must be chosen, what needed all this circuit and caution, to do that which is not possible to be done otherwise, which one may do as well as a thousand, and for doing of which no rationall man can be offended, if the Electors were necessarily predetermined to elect this man and no other. And though *T. H.* was pleased to passe by my University

versity instance, yet I may not, untill I see what he is able to say unto it. The Junior of the Mess in *Cambridge* divides the meat into foure parts, The Senior chooseth first, then the second and third in their order. The Junior is determined to one, and hath no choise left, unless it be to choose whether he will take that part which the rest have refused, or none at all. It may be this part is more agreable to his mind than any of the others would have been, but for all that he cannot be said to choose it, because he is determined to this one. Even such a liberty of election is that which is established by *T. H.* Or rather much worse in two respects. The Junior hath yet a liberty of contradiction left to choose whether he will take that part or not take any part, but he who is precisely predetermined to the choise of this object, hath no liberty to refuse it. Secondly, the Junior by dividing carefully may preserve to himself an equall share, but he who is wholly determined by extrinsecall causes, is left altogether to the mercy and disposition of another.

3   Thirdly, I proove it by the texts alledged, *Numb.* 30. 13. If a wife make a vow, it is left to her husbands choise, either to establish it or make it void. But if it be predetermined, that he shall establish it, it is not in his power to make it void. If it be predetermined, that he shall make it void, it is not in his power to establish it. And howsoever it be determined, yet being determined, it is not in his power indifferently, either to establish it, or to make it void

at

at his pleasure. So Joshua 24.15. *Choose you this day whom ye will serve: But I and my house will serve the Lord.* It is too late to choose that *this day*, which was determined otherwise yesterday, *whom ye will serve, whether the gods whom your fathers served, or the gods of the Amorites.* Where there is an election of this or that, these gods, or those gods, there must needs be either an indifferency to both objects, or at least a possibility of either. *I and my house will serve the Lord.* If he were extrinsecally predetermined, he should not say I will serve, but I must serve. And 2 Sam. 24. 12. *I offer thee three things, choose thee which of them I shall do.* How doth God offer three things to *Davids* choise, if he had predetermined him to one of the three by a concourse of necessary extrinsecall causes? If a soveraign Prince should descend so far as to offer a delinquent his choice, whether he would be fined, or imprisoned, or banished, and had under hand signed the sentence of his banishment, what were it els but plain drollery, or mockery? This is the argument which in *T. H.* his opinion looks another way. If it do, it is as the *Parthians* used to fight, flying. His reason followes next to be considered.

T. H.

Numb. 7.

For if there come into the husbands mind greater good by establishing than abrogating such a vow, the establishing will follow necessarily. And if the evill that will follow thereon in the husbands opinion outweigh the good, the contrary must needs follow. And yet in this following of ones hopes and feares consisteth the nature of election. So that a man may both choose this, and cannot but choose this. And consequently choosing and necessity are joyned together.

J. D.

THere is nothing said with more shew of reason in this cause by the patrons of necessity, and adversaries of true liberty than this, That the will doth perpetually and infallibly follow the last dictate of the understanding, or the last judgment of right reason. And in this, and this onely, I confess *T. H.* hath good seconds. Yet the common and approved opinion is contrary. And justly: For,

First, this very act of the understanding is an effect of the will, and a testimony of its power and liberty. It is the will, which affecting some particular good doth, ingage and command the understanding to consult and deliberate what means are convenient for atteining that end. And though the will it self be blind, yet its object is good in generall, which is the end of all human actions. Therefore it belongs to the will as to the Generall of an Army to moove the other powers of the soul to their acts, and among the rest the understanding also, by applying it and reducing its power into act. So as whatsoever obligation the understanding doth put upon the will, is by the consent of the will, and derived from the power of the will, which was not necessitated to moove the understanding to consult. So the will is the Lady and Mistris of human actions, the understanding is her trusty counseller, which gives no advise, but when it is required by the will. And if the first consultation or deliberation be not sufficient, the will may moove a review, and require the understanding to inform it self better, and take advise of others, from whence many times the judgment of the understanding doth receive alteration.

Secondly, for the manner how the understanding doth determine the will, it is not naturally but morally. The will is mooved by the understanding, not as by an efficient, having a causall influence into the effect, but only by proposing and representing the object. And therefore as it were ridiculous to say, that the object of the sight is the cause of seeing, so it is to say, that the proposing of the object by the understanding to the will, is the cause of willing; and therefore the understanding hath no place in that concourse of causes which according to *T. H.* do necessitate the will.

Thirdly, the judgment of the understanding is not alwayes *practicè practicum*, nor of such a nature in it self, as to oblige and determine the will to one. Sometimes the understanding proposeth two or three means equally available to the altering of one and the same end. Sometimes it dictateth, that this or that particular good is eligible or fit to be chosen, but not that it is necessarily eligible, or that it must be chosen. It may judge this or that to be a fit means, but not the onely meanes to atteine the desired end. In these cases no man can doubt, but that the will

will may choose, or not choose, this or that indifferently. Yea, though the understanding shall judge one of these means to be more expedient than another, yet for as much as in the less expedient there is found the reason of good, the will in respect of that dominion which it hath over it self, may accept that which the understanding judgeth to be less expedient, and refuse that which it judgeth to be more expedient.

4 Fourthly, sometimes the will doth not will the end so efficaciously, but that it may be, and often is deterred from the prosecution of it by the difficulty of the means; and notwithstanding the judgment of the understanding, the will may still suspend its own act.

5 Fiftly, supposing but not granting, that the will did necessarily follow the last dictate of the understanding, yet this prooves no antecedent necessity, but coexistent with the act, no extrinsecall necessity, the will and understanding being but two faculties of the same soul, no absolute necessity, but meerly upon supposition. And therefore the same Authors who maintain that the judgment of the understanding doth necessarily determine the will, do yet much more earnestly oppugne *T. H.* his absolute necessity of all occurrences. Suppose the will shall apply the understanding to deliberate and not require a review. Suppose the dictate of the understanding shall be absolute, not this or that indifferently, nor this rather than that comparatively, but this positively, not this freely, but this necessarily. And suppose the will do well efficaciously,

ously, and do not suspend its own act. Then here is a necessity indeed, but neither absolute, nor extrinsecall, nor antecedent, flowing from a concourse of causes without our selves, but a necessity upon supposition, which we do readily grant. So far *T. H.* is wide from the truth, whilest he mainteines, either that the apprehension of a greater good doth necessitate the will, or that this is an absolute necessity.

Lastly, whereas he saith, that *the nature of election doth consist in following our hopes and feares*, I cannot but observe that there is not one word of Art in this whole Treatise, which he useth in the right sense; I hope it doth not proceed out of an affectation of singularity, nor out of a contempt of former Writers, nor out of a desire to take in sunder the whole frame of Learning, and new mould it after his own mind. It were to be wished that at least he would give us a new Dictionary, that we might understand his sense. But because this is but touched here sparingly and upon the by, I will forbear it, untill I meet with it again in its proper place. And for the present it shall suffice to say, that hopes and feares are common to brute beasts, but election is a rationall act, and is proper only to man, who is *Sanctius his animal mentisq; capacius altæ.*

T. H.

THE *second place of Scripture is* Josh. 24. 15. *The third is* 2 Sam. 24. 12. *whereby tis cleerely prooved, that there is election in man, but not prooved that such election was not necessitated stated by the hopes, and feares, and considerations of good and bad to follow, which depend not on the will, nor are subject to election. And therefore one answer serves all such places, if they were a thousand.*

J. D.

THis answer being the very same with the former, word for word, which hath already been sufficiently shaken in pieces, doth require no new reply.

T. H.

Numb. 8. *SUpposing, it seemes, I might answer as I have done, that necessity and election might stand together, and instance in the actions of Children, fools, and brute beasts, whose fancies I might say, are necessitated and determined to one: before these his proofs out of Scripture he desires to prevent that instance, and therefore sayes, that the actions of children, fools, mad-men and beasts are indeed determined, but that they proceed not from election, nor from free, but from spontaneous Agents. As for example, that the Bee when it maketh honey does it spontaneously; And when the Spider makes his webb, he does it spontaneously, and not by election. Though I never meant to ground any answer upon the experience of what Children, foools, mad-men and beasts do, yet that your Lordship may understand what can be meant by spontaneous, and how it differs from voluntary, I will answer that distinction and shew, that it fighteth against its fellow Arguments. Your Lordship is therefore to consider, that all voluntary actions, where the thing that*

induceth

induceth the will is not fear, are called also spontaneous, and said to be done by a mans own accord. As *when a man giveth money voluntarily to another for merchandise, or out of affection, he is said to do it of his own accord, which in* Latin *is* Sponte, *and therefore the action is spontaneous. Though to give ones money willingly to a thief to avoid killing, or throw it into the Sea to avoid drowning, where the motive is fear, be not called spontaneous. But every spontaneous action is not therfore voluntary, for voluntary presupposes some precedent deliberation, that is to say, some consideration and meditation of what is likely to follow, both upon the doing and abstaining from the action deliberated of, whereas many actions are done of our own accord, and be therefore spontaneous ; of which neverthelesse as he thinks we never consulted, nor deliberated of in our selves, as when making no question, nor any the least doubt in the world, but that the thing we are about is good, we eat, or walk, or in anger strike or revile, which he thinks spontaneous, but not voluntary nor elective actions. And with such kind of actions he sayes necessitation may stand, but not from such as are voluntary, and proceed upon election and deliberation. Now if I make it appear to you, that even these actions which he sayes proceed from spontaneity, and which he ascribes only to fools,* Children, *mad-men, and beasts, proceed from deliberation and election, and that actions inconsiderate, rash and spontaneous are ordinarily found in those that are by themselves, and many more thought as wise or wiser than ordinary*

dinary men are. Then his Argument concludeth, that necessity and election may stand together, which is contrary to that which he intendeth by all the rest of his Arguments to proove. And first your Lordships own experience furnishes you with proof enough, that horses, doggs, and other brute beasts do demurre oftentimes upon the way they are to take. The horse retiring from some strange figure he sees, and comming on again to avoid the spur. And what els does man that deliberateth, but one while proceed toward action, another while retire from it, as the hope of greater good drawes him, or the fear of greater evill drives him? A Child may be so young as to do all which it does without all deliberation, but that is but till it chance to be hurt by doing somewhat, or till it be of age to understand the rod; for the actions wherein he hath once a check, shall be deliberated on the second time. Fools and mad-men manifestly deliberate no less then the wisest men, though they make not so good a cloise, the images of things, being by diseases altered. For Bees and Spiders, if he had so little to do as to be a spectator of their actions, he would have confessed not onely Election, but also Art, Prudence, and Policy in them, very neer equall to that of mankind. Of Bees, Aristotle sayes, their life is civill. He is deceived, if he think any spontaneous action after once being checked in it, differs from an action voluntary and elective, for even the setting of a mans foot in the posture of walking, and the action of ordinary eating, was once deliberated, how and when it should be done; And though it

afterward

afterward become easy and habitual, so as to be done without fore-thought, yet that does not hinder, but that the act is voluntary, and proceeds from election. So also are the rashest actions of cholerick persons voluntary and upon deliberation; for who is there but very young Children, that has not considered, when and how far he ought or safely may, strike or revile, seeing then he agrees with me that such actions are necessitated, and the fancy of those that do them is determined to the actions they do, it follows out of his own doctrin, that the liberty of election does not take away the necessity of electing, this or that individuall thing. And thus one of his Arguments fights against another.

J. D.

WE have partly seen before how *T. H.* hath coined a new kind of liberty, a new kind of necessity, a new kind of election, and now in this section a new kind of spontaneity, and a new kind of voluntary actions. Although he say, that here is nothing new to him, yet I begin to suspect, that either here are many things new to him, or otherwise his election is not the result of a serious mature deliberation. The first thing that I offer, is, how often he mistakes my meaning in this one section; first, I make voluntary and spontaneous actions to be one and the same, he saith I distinguish them, so as spontaneous actions may be necessary, but voluntary actions cannot. Secondly, I distinguish between free acts and voluntary acts. The former are alwaies deliberate, the latter may be indeliberate; all free acts are voluntary, but all voluntary acts are not free, but he saith I confound them and make them the same. Thirdly, he saith I ascribe spontaneity onely to Fools, Children, Mad-Men and Beasts, But I acknowledge spontaneity hath place in rationall men, both as it is comprehended in liberty, and as it is distinguished from liberty.

Yet I have no reason to be offended at it; for he deals no otherwise with me then he doth with himself. Here he tells us, that *voluntary, præsupposeth deliberation.* But Numb. 25. he tells us contrary, *that whatsoever followeth the last appetite is voluntary, and where there is but one appetite, that is the last.* And that *no action of a man can be said to be without deliberation, though never so suddain.* So Numb. 33. he tells us, that *by spontaneity is meant, inconsiderate proceeding, or else nothing is meant by it*, yet here he tells us, that *all voluntary actions which proceed not from fear, are spontaneous*, whereof many are deliberate, as that wherein he instanceth himself, *to give mony for merchandise.* Thirdly, when I said that Children before they have the use of reason, act spontaneously, as when they suck the Breast, but do not act freely because they have not judgement to deliberate or elect, Here *T. H.* undertakes to proove, that they do deliberate and elect. And yet presently after confesseth again, that *a Child may be so young, as to do what it doth without all deliberation.*

3. Besides these mistakes and contradictions he hath other errours also in this section. As this, that

that no actions proceeding from fear are spontaneous. He who throws his goods into the Sea, to avoid drowning doth it not onely *spontaneously* but even *freely*, He that wills the end, wills the means conducing to that end. It is true that if the action be considered nakedly without all circumstances, no man willingly or spontaneously casts his goods into the Sea. But if we take the action as in this particular case invested with all the circumstances, and in order to the end, that is, the saving of his own life, it is not onely voluntary and spontaneous, but elective and chosen by him, as the most probable means for his own preservation. As there is an Antecedent and a subsequent will, so there is an Antecedent and a subsequent spontaneity: His Grammaticall argument, grounded upon the derivation of spontaneous from *sponte*, weighs nothing; we have learned in the rudiments of Logick that conjugates are sometimes in name onely, and not indeed. He who casts his goods in the Sea, may do it of his own accord in order to the end. Secondly, he erres in this also, that nothing is opposed to spontaneity but onely fear. Invincible and Antecedent ignorance doth destroy the nature of spontaneity or voluntarines, by removing that knowledge which should and would have prohibited the action. As a man thinking to shoot a wild Beast in a Bush, shoots his friend, which if he had known, he would not have shot. This man did not kill his friend of his own accord.

For the clearer understanding of these things, and

and to know what spontaneity is, let us consult a while with the Schools about the distinct order of voluntary or involuntary actions. Some acts proceed wholy from an extrinsecall cause; as the throwing of a stone upwards, a rape, or the drawing of a Christian by plain force to the Idols Temple, these are called violent acts. Secondly, some proceed from an intrinsecall cause, but without any manner of knowledge of the end, as the falling of a stone downwards, these are called naturall acts. Thirdly, some proceed from an internall principle, with an imperfect knowledge of the end, where there is an appetite to the object, but no deliberation nor election, as the acts of Fools, Children, Beasts, and the inconsiderate acts of men of judgement. These are called voluntary or spontaneous acts. Fourthly, some proceed from an intrinsecal cause, with a more perfect knowledge of the end, which are elected upon deliberation. These are called free acts. So then the formall reason of liberty is election. The necessary requisite to election is deliberation. Deliberation implieth the actuall use of reason. But deliberation and election cannot possibly subsist, with an extrinsecall prædetermination to one. How should a man deliberate or choose which way to go, who knows that all wayes are shut against him, and made impossible to him, but onely one? This is the genuine sense of these words *voluntary* and *spontaneous* in this question. Though they were taken twenty other wayes vulgarly or metaphorically, as we say

say *spontaneous ulcers*, where there is no appetite at all, yet it were nothing to this controversy, which is not about Words, but about Things; not what the words Voluntary or Free do or may signifie, but whether all things be extrinsecally præcdetermined to one.

These grounds being laid for clearing the true sense of the words, the next thing to be examined is, that contradiction which he hath espied in my discourse, or how this Argument fights against its fellows. If I (saith *T. H.*) make it appear, that the spontaneous actions of Fools, Children, Mad-Men and Beasts, do proceed from election and deliberation, and that inconsiderate and indeliberate actions are found in the wisest men, then his argument concludes, that necessity and election may stand together, which is contrary to his assertion. If this could be made appear as easily as it is spoken, it would concern himself much, who when he should proove, that rationall men are not free from necessity, goes about to proove that brute Beasts do deliberate and elect, that is as much as to say, are free from necessity. But it concerns not me at all, It is neither my assertion, nor my opinion, that necessity and election may not meet together in the same subject, violent, naturall, spontaneous, and deliberate or elective acts may all meet together in the same subject. But this I say, that necessity and election cannot consist together in the same act. He who is determined to one, is not free to choose out of more then one. To begin

begin with his latter suppoſition, *that wiſe men may do inconſiderate and indeliberate actions*, I do readily admit it. But where did he learn to infer a generall concluſion from particular premiſſes? as thus, becauſe wiſe men do ſome indeliberate acts, therefore no act they do is free or elective. Secondly, for his former ſuppoſition, *That fools, children, mad-men, and beaſts do deliberate and elect*, if he could make it good, it is not I who contradict my ſelf, nor fight againſt mine own aſſertion, but it is he who endevours to proove that which I altogether deny. He may well find a contradiction between him and me, otherwiſe to what end is this diſpute? But he ſhall not be able to find a difference between me and my ſelf: But the truth is, he is not able to proove any ſuch thing; and that brings me to my ſixth Conſideration.

6   That neither Horſes, nor Bees, nor Spiders, nor Children, nor Fools, nor Mad-men do deliberate or elect. His firſt inſtance is in the Horſe or Dog, but more eſpecially the Horſe. He told me, that I divided my argument into ſquadrons, to apply my ſelf to your Lordſhip, being a Military man; And I apprehend, that for the ſame reaſon he gives his firſt inſtance of the Horſe, with a ſubmiſſion to your own experience. So far well, but otherwiſe very diſadvantagiouſly to his cauſe. Men uſe to ſay of a dull fellow, that he hath no more braines than an horſe. And the Prophet *David* ſaith, *Be not like the Horſe and Mule which have no underſtanding*. Pſal. 32. 9. How do they deliberate without underſtanding?

ding? And Psal. 49. 20. he saith the same of all brute beasts. *Man being in honour had no understanding, but became like unto the beasts that perish.* The horse *demurres upon his way*, Why not? Outward objects, or inward fancies may produce a stay in his course, though he have no judgment, either to deliberate or elect. *He retires from some strange figure which he sees, and comes on again to avoid the spur.* So he may, and yet be far enough from deliberation. All this proceeds from the sensitive passion of fear, which is a perturbation arising from the expectation of some imminent evill. But he urgeth, what els doth man that deliberateth? Yes very much. The horse feareth some outward object, but deliberation is a comparing of severall means conducing to the same end. Fear is commonly of one, deliberation of more than one; fear is of those things which are not in our power, deliberation of those things which are in our power; fear ariseth many times out of naturall antipathies, but in these disconveniences of nature, deliberation hath no place at all. In a word, fear is an enemy to deliberation, and betrayeth the succours of the Soul. If the horse did deliberate, he should consult with reason, whether it were more expedient for him to go that way or not; He should represent to himself, all the dangers both of going, and staying, and compare the one with the other, and elect that which is less evill; He should consider whether it were not better to endure a little hazard, than ungratefully and dishonestly to fail in his duty to his master, who did breed

breed him, and doth feed him. This the horse doth not; Neither is it possible for him to do it. Secondly, for Children, *T. H.* confesseth that they may be so young, that they do not deliberate at all; Afterwards, as they attein to the use of reason by degrees, so by degrees they become free agents. Then they do deliberate, before they do not deliberate. The rod may be a means to make them use their reason, when they have power to exercise it, but the rod cannot produce the power before they have it. Thirdly, for fools and mad-men. It is not to be understood of such mad-men as have their *lucida intervalla*, who are mad and discreet by fitts; when they have the use of reason, they are no mad-men, but may deliberate as well as others. Nor yet of such fools as are only comparative fools, that is, less wise than others. Such may deliberate, though not so clearly, nor so judiciously as others, but of meer mad-men, and meer naturall fools, to say that they, who have not the use of reason, do deliberate or use reason, implies a contradiction. But his chiefest confidence is in his Bees and Spiders, *of whose actions* (he saith) *if I had been a spectator, I would have confessed, not only Election, but also Art, Prudence, Policy, very neer equall to that of mankind, whose life, as* Aristotle *saith, is civill.* Truly I have contemplated their actions many times, and have been much taken with their curious works, yet my thoughts did not reflect so much upon them, as upon their maker, who is *sic magnus in magnis*, that he is not, *minor in parvis*

parvis. So great in great things, that he is not less in small things. Yes, I have seen those sillieſt of creatures, and ſeeing their rare works, I have seen enough to confute all the bold-faced Atheiſts of this age, and their helliſh blaſphemies. I ſee them, but I praiſed the marveillous works of God, and admired that great and firſt intellect, who had both adapted their organs, and determined their fancies to theſe particular works. I was not ſo ſimple to aſcribe thoſe Rarities to their own invention, which I knew to proceed from a meer inſtinct of Nature. In all other things they are the dulleſt of creatures. Naturaliſts write of Bees, that their fancy is imperfect, not diſtinct from their common ſenſe, ſpread over their whole body, and only perceiving things preſent. When *Ariſtotle* calls them Politicall or Sociable Creatures, he did not intend it really that they lived a civill life, but according to an Analogy, becauſe they do ſuch things by inſtinct, as truly Politicall Creatures do out of judgment. Nor when I read in St. *Ambroſe*, of their *Hexagonies* or *Sexangular* celler, did I therefore conclude, that they were *Mathematicians*. Nor when I read in *Creſpet*, that they invoke God to their aid, when they go out of their Hives, bending their thighs in forme of a croſs, and bowing themſelves; did I therefore think, that this was an act of religious piety, or that they were capable of *Theologicall* vertues, whom I ſee in all other things in which their fancies are not determined, to be the ſillieſt of creatures, ſtrangers not only to right reaſon,

but

but to all resemblances of it.

7 Seventhly, concerning those actions which are done upon precedent and passed deliberations; They are not only spontaneous, but free acts. Habits contracted by use and experience do help the will to act with more facility, and more determinately, as the hand of the Artificer is helped by his tools. And precedent deliberations, if they were sad and serious, and prooved by experience to be profitable, do save the labour of subsequent consultations, *frustra fit per plura, quod fieri potest per pauciora*, yet neverthelesss the actions which are done by vertue of these formerly acquired habits are no less free, then if the deliberation were coexistent with this particular action. He that hath gained an habit and skill to play such a lesson, needs not a new deliberation how to play every time that he playes it over and over; yet I am far from giving credit to him in this, that walking or eating universally considered are free actions, or proceed from true liberty, not so much because they want a particular deliberation before every individuall act, as because they are animall motions, and need no deliberation of reason, as we see in brute beasts. And nevertheless the same actions, as they are considered individually, and invested with their due circumstances, may be and often are free actions subverted to the liberty of the Agent.

8 Lastly, whereas *T. H.* compareth the first motions or rash attempts of cholerick persons with such acquired habits, it is a great mistake,

Those

Those rash attempts are voluntary actions, and may be facilitated sometimes by acquired habits; But yet for as much as actions are often altered and varied by the circumstances of Time, Place and Person, so as that act which at one time is morally good, at another time may be morally evill. And for as much as a generall precedent deliberation how to do this kind of action is not sufficient to make this or that particular action good or expedient, which being in it self good, yet particular circumstances may render inconvenient or unprofitable, to some persons, at some times, in some places. Therefore a precedent generall deliberation how to do any act, as for instance, how to write, is not sufficient to make a particular act, as my writing this individuall reply to be freely done, without a particular and subsequent deliberation. A man learnes *French* advisedly, that is a free act: The same man in his choler and passion reviles his friend in *French*, without any deliberation, This is a spontaneous act, but it is not a free act; If he had taken time to advise, he would not have reviled his friend. Yet as it is not free, so neither is it so necessary, as the Bees making hony, whose fancy is not only inclined but determined by nature to that act. So every way he failes. And his conclusion, that the liberty of Election, doth not take away the necessity of electing this or that individuall thing, is no consequent from my doctrine, but from his own. Neither do my arguments fight one against another, but his private opinions fight

fight both againſt me and againſt an undoubted truth. A free agent endowed with liberty of election, or with an elective power, may nevertheleſs be neceſſitated in ſome individuall acts, but thoſe acts wherein he is neceſſitated, do not flow from his elective power, neither are thoſe acts which flow from his elective power neceſſitated.

J. D.

Numb. 9. Arg. 2. Secondly, they who might have done, and may do many things which they leave undone; And they who leave undone many things which they might do, are neither compelled nor neceſſitated to do what they do, but have true liberty. But we might do many things which we do not, and we do many things which we might leave undone, as is plain, 1 King. 3. 11. *Becauſe thou haſt asked this thing, and haſt not asked for thy ſelf long life, neither haſt asked riches for thy ſelf, nor haſt asked the life of thine enemies, &c.* God gave *Salomon* his choiſe. He might have asked riches, but then he had not asked wiſedom, which he did ask. He did ask wiſedom, but he might have asked riches, which yet he did not ask. And Act. 5. 4. *After it was ſold, was it not in thine own power?* It was in his own power to give it, and it was in his own power to retein it. Yet if he did give it he could not retein it; And if he did retein it, he could not give it. Therefore we may do, what we do not. And we do not, what we might do. That is, we have true liberty from neceſſity.

T. H.

T. H.

THE second argument from Scripture consisteth in Histories of men, that did one thing, when if they would they might have done another. The places are two, one is in the 1 Kings 3. 11. Where the history sayes, God was pleased that Salomon, who might, if he would, have asked riches or revenge, did nevertheless ask wisedom at Gods hands. The other is the words of St. Peter to Ananias, Act. 5. 4. After it was sold, was it not in thine own power?

To which the answer is the same, with that I answered to the former places. That they proove there is election, but do not disproove the necessity which I maintain of what they so elect.

J. D.

WE have had the very same answer twice before. It seemeth that he is well pleased with it, or els he would not draw it in again so suddenly by head and shoulders, to no purpose, if he did not conceive it to be a Panchreston, a salve for all sores, or *Dictamnum*, soveraign Dittany, to make all his adversaries weapons drop out of the wounds of his cause, onely by chewing it, without any application to the sore. I will not wast the time to shew any further, how the members of his distinction do cross one another, and one take away another. To make every election to be of one thing imposed by necessity, and of another thing which is absolutely impossible, is to make election to be no election at all. But I forbear to press that in present. If I may be bold to use his own phrase; His answer fwer looks quite another way from mine Argument. My second reason was this, They who may do, and might have done many things which they leave undone, and who leave undone many things which they might do, are not necessitated, nor precisely, and antecently determined to do what they do.

But we might do many things which we do not, and we do many things which we might leave undone, as appeares evidently by the texts alledged. Therefore we are not antecedently and precisely determined, nor necessitated to do all things which he do. What is here of *election* in this Argument? To what proposition, to what tearm doth *T. H.* apply his answer? He neither affirmes, nor denieth, nor distinguisheth of any thing contained in my argument. Here I must be bold to call upon him for a more pertinent answer.

J. D.

Numb. 10.
Arg. 3.

THirdly, if there be no true liberty, but all things come to pass by inevitable necessity, then what are all those interrogations, and objurgations, and reprehensions, and expostulations which we find so frequently in holy Scriptures, (be it spoken with all due respect) but feined and hypocriticall exaggerations? *Hast thou eaten of the tree whereof I commanded that thou shouldest not eat?* Gen. 3. 11. And ver. 13. he saith to Eve, *Why hast thou done this?* And to Cain, *Why art thou wroth, and why is thy countenance cast down? And why will ye dy, O house of Israel?* Doth God command openly not to eat,

eat, and yet secretly by himself or by the second causes necessitate him to eat? Doth he reprehend him for doing that, which he hath antecedently determined that he must doe? Doth he propose things under impossible conditions? Or were not this plain mockery and derision? Doth a loving Master chide his servant, because he doth not come at his call, and yet knowes that the poor servant is chained and fettered, so as he cannot moove, by the Masters own order, without the servants default or consent? They who talk here of a twofold will of God, *secret* and *revealed*, and the one opposite to the other, understand not what they say. These two wills concerne severall persons. The secret will of God is what he will do himself; The revealed will of God is what he would have us to do; It may be the secret will of God to take away the life of the Father, yet it is Gods revealed will that his Son should wish his life, and pray for his life. Here is no contradiction where the Agents are distinct. But for the same person to command one thing, and yet to necessitate him that is commanded to do another thing; To chide a man for doing that, which he hath determined inevitably and irresistibly that he must do; This were (I am afraid to utter what they are not afraid to assert) the highest dissimulation. Gods chiding prooves mans liberty.

T. H.

(52)

T. H.

TO the third and fift arguments, I shall make but one answer.

J. D.

CErtainly distinct Arguments, as the third and fift are, the one drawn from the truth of God, the other drawn from the Justice of God, the one from his objurgations and reprehensions, the other from his Judgments after life, did require distinct answers. But the plain truth is, that neither here, nor in his answer to the fift Argument, nor in this whole Treatise, is there one word of solution or satisfaction to this Argument, or to any part of it. All that looks like an answer is contained, Numb. 12. *That which he does, is made just by his doing, Just I say, in him, not alwayes just in us by the example; for a man that shall command a thing openly, and plot secretly the hinderance of the same, if he punish him whom he commanded so, for not doing it, is unjust:* I dare no insist upon it, I hope his meaning is not so bad as the words intimate, and as I apprehend, That is to impute falshood to him that is Truth it self, and to justifie feining and dissimulation in God, as he doth tyranny, by the infiniteness of his power, and the absoluteness of his dominion. And therefore by his leave, I must once again tender him a new summons for a full and clear Answer to this Argument also. He tells us, that he was not surprised. Whether he were or not, is more than I know. But this I see plainly, that either he is not provided, or that his cause admits no choise

of

of answers. The Jews dealt ingenuously when they met with a difficult knot, which they could not untie, to put it upon *Elias*. Elias *will answer it when he comes.*

J. D.

FOurthly, if either the decree of God, or the foreledge of God, or the influence of the Stars, or the concatenation of causes, or the physicall, or morall efficacy of objects, or the last dictate of the understanding, do take away true liberty, then *Adam* before his fall had no true liberty. For he was subjected to the same decrees, the same præscience, the same constellations, the same causes, the same objects, the same dictates of the understanding. But, *quicquid ostendes mihi sic incredulus odi*, The greatest opposers of our liberty, are as earnest maintainers of the liberty of *Adam*. Therefore none of these supposed impediments take away true liberty.

Numb. 11.
Arg. 4.

T. H.

THe fourth Argument is to this effect, *If the decree of God, or his foreknowledge, or the influence of the Stars, or the concatenation of causes, or the physicall, or morall efficacy of causes, or the last dictate of the understanding, or whatsoever it be, do take away true liberty, then* Adam *before his fall had no true liberty,* Quicquid ostendes mihi sic incredulus odi. *That which I say necessitateth and determinateth every action, that he may no longer doubt of my meaning, is the sum of all those things, which being now existent, conduce and concurre to the* production of that action hereafter, whereof if any one thing now were wanting, the effect could not be produced. This concourse of causes, whereof every one is determined to be such, as it is by a like concourse of former causes, may well be called (in respect they were all set and ordered by the eternall cause of all things God Almighty) the decree of God.

But that the fore-knowledge of God, should be a cause of any thing, cannot be truly said, seeing foreknowledge is knowledge, and knowledge depends on the existence of the things known, and not they on it.

The influence of the Stars is but a small part of the whole cause, consisting of the concourse of all Agents.

Nor doth the concourse of all causes make one simple chain, or concatenation, but an innumerable number of chains joyned together, not in all parts, but in the first link, God Almighty; and consequently the whole cause of an event, does not alwaies depend upon one single chain, but on many together.

Naturall efficacy of objects does determine voluntary Agents, and necessitates the will, and consequently the action; but for morall efficacy, I understand not what he means by it. The last dictate of the judgement concerning the good or bad that may follow on any action, is not properly the whole cause, but the last part of it. And yet may be said to produce the effect necessarily, in such manner as the last feather may be said to break an Horses back, when there were

were so many laid on before, as there wanted but that to do it.

Now for his *Argument*, That if the concourse of all the causes necessitate the effect, that then it follows, Adam had no true liberty. I deny the consequence, for I make not onely the effect, but also the election of that particular effect to be necessary, in as much as the will it self, and each propension of a man during his deliberation is as much necessitated, and depends on a sufficient cause, as any thing else whatsoever. As for example, it is no more necessary that fire should burn, then that a man, or other creature, whose limbs be moved by fancy, should have election, that is, liberty to do what he has a fancy to, though it be not in his will or power to choose his fancy, or choose his election or will.

This *Doctrin*, because he saies he hates, I doubt had better been suppressed, as it should have been, if both your Lordship, and he had not pressed me to an answer.

J. D.

THis Argument was sent forth onely as an espie to make a more full discovery, what were the true grounds of *T. H.* his supposed necessity; which errand being done, and the foundation whereupon he builds being found out, which is as I called it a concatenation of causes, and as he calles it a concourse of necessary causes; It would now be a superfluous, and impertinent work in me to undertake the refutation of all those other opinions, which he doth not undertake to defend. And therefore

fore I shall wave them for the present, with these short animadversions.

Concerning the eternall decree of God, he confounds the decree it self with the execution of his decree. And concerning the fore-knowledge of God, he confounds that speculative knowledge, which is called *the knowledge of vision*, which doth not produce the intellective objects, no more then the sensitive vision doth produce the sensible objects, with that other knowledge of God, which is called the *knowledge of approbation*, or *a practicall knowledge*, that is, knowledge joyned with an act of the will, of which Divines do truly say, that it is the cause of things, as the knowledge of the Artist is the cause of his work. God made all things by his word, *Joh.* 1. that is, by his wisdom. Concerning the influences of the Stars, I wish he had expressed himself more clearly; For as I do willingly grant, that those Heavenly Bodies do act upon these sublunary things, not onely by their motion and light, but also by an occult vertue, which we call influence, as we see by manifold experience in the Loadstone, and Shell-fish, &c. So if he intend, that by these influences they do naturally or physically determine the will, or have any direct dominion over humane Counsels, either in whole or in part, either more or less, he is in an errour. Concerning the concatenation of causes, whereas he makes not one chain, but an innumerable number of chains, (I hope he speaks hyperbolically, and doth not intend that they are actually infinite,) the difference

is

is not materiall whether one or many, so long as they are all joyned together, both in the first linck, and likewise in the effect. It serves to no end, but to shew what a shadow of liberty *T. H.* doth fancy, or rather what a dream of a shadow. As if one chain were not sufficient to load poor man, but he must be clogged with innumerable chains. This is just such another freedom, as the Turkish Galli-slaves do injoy. But I admire that *T. H.* who is so versed in this question, should here confess, that he understands not the difference between physicall, or naturall, and morall efficacy. And much more, that he should affirm, that outward objects do determine voluntary agents by a naturall efficacy. No object, no second agent, Angell or Devill, can determine the will of man naturally, but God alone, in respect of his supreme dominion over all things. Then the will is determined naturally, when God Almighty, besides his generall influence, whereupon all second causes do depend, as well for their being as for their acting, doth moreover at sometimes, when it pleaseth him in cases extraordinary, concurre by a speciall influence, and infuse something into the will, in the nature of an act, or an habit, whereby the will is moved, and excited, and applied to will or choose this or that. Then the will is determined morally, when some object is proposed to it with perswasive reasons and arguments to induce it to will. Where the determination is naturall, the liberty to suspend its act is taken away

away from the will, but not so where the determination is morall. In the former case, the will is determined extrinsecally, in the latter case intrinsecally; The former produceth an absolute necessity, the latter onely a necessity of supposition. If the will do not suspend, but assent, then the act is necessary; but because the will may suspend and not assent, therefore it is not absolutely necessary. In the former case the will is moved necessarily and determinately, In the latter freely and indeterminately. The former excitation is immediate, the latter is *mediate mediante intellectu*, and requires the help of the understanding. In a word, so great a difference there is between naturall and morall efficacy, as there is between his opinion and mine in this question.

There remains onely the last dictate of the understanding, which he maketh to be the last cause that concerneth to the determination of the will, and to the necessary production of the act, *as the last feather may be said to break an Horses back, when there were so many laid on before, that there wanted but that to do it.* I have shewed *Numb.* 7. that the last dictate of the understanding, is not alwaies absolute in it self, nor conclusive to the will, and when it is conclusive, yet it produceth no Antecedent nor Extrinsecall necessity; I shall onely adde one thing more in present, That by making the last judgement of right reason to be of no more weight then a single feather, he wrongs the understanding as well as he doth the will, the
indea-

indeavours to deprive the will of its supreme power of application, and to deprive the understanding of its supreme power of judicature and definition. Neither corporeall agents and objects, nor yet the sensitive appetite it self, being an inferiour faculty, and affixed to the Organ of the Body, have any direct or immediate dominion or command over the rationall will. It is without the sphear of their activity. All the accefs which they have unto the will, is by the means of the understanding, sometimes clear, and sometimes disturbed, and of reason either right or mif-informed. Without the help of the understanding, all his second causes were not able of themselves to load the Horses back with so much weight as the least of all his feathers doth amount unto. But we shall meet with his Horse load of feathers again *Num.* 23.

These things being thus briefly touched, he proceeds to his answer. My argument was this, If any of these, or all of these causes formerly recited, do take away true liberty, (that is, still intended from necessity) then *Adam* before his fall had no true liberty.

But *Adam* before his fall had true liberty.

He mif-recites the argument, and denies the consequence, which is so clearly proved, that no man living can doubt of it. Because *Adam* was subjected to all the same causes as well as we, the same decree, the same præscience, the same influences, the same concourse of causes, the same efficacy of objects, the same dictates of reason. But it is onely a mistake, for it appears

pears plainly by his following discourse, that he intended to deny, not the consequence, but the Assumption; For he makes *Adam* to have had no liberty from necessity before his fall, yea he proceeds so far, as to affirm, that all humane wills, his and ours, and each propension of our wills, even during our deliberation, are as much necessitated as any thing else whatsoever; that we have no more power to forbear those actions which we do, then the fire hath power not to burn. Though I honour *T. H.* for his person, and for his learning, yet I must confess ingenuously, I hate this Doctrin from my heart. And I beleeve both I have reason so to do, and all others who shall seriously ponder the horrid consequences which flow from it. It destroyes liberty, and dishonours the nature of man. It makes the second causes and outward objects to be the Rackets, and Men to be but the Tennis-Balls of destiny. It makes the first cause, that is, God Almighty, to be the introducer of all evill, and sin into the world, as much as Man, yea more then Man, by as much as the motion of the Watch is more from the Artificer, who did make it and wind it up, then either from the spring, or the wheels, or the thred, if God by his speciall influence into the second causes, did necessitate them to operate as they did. And if they being thus determined, did necessitate *Adam* inevitably, irresistibly, not by an accidentall, but by an essentiall subordination of causes to whatsoever he did, Then one of these two absurdities must needs

needs follow, either that *Adam* did not sin, and that there is no such thing as sin in the world, because it proceeds naturally, necessarily, and essentially from God. Or that God is more guilty of it, and more the cause of evill than man, because man is extrinsecally, inevitably determined, but so is not God. And in causes essentially subordinate, the cause of the cause is always the cause of the effect. What Tyrant did ever impose Lawes that were impossible for those to keep upon whom they were imposed, and punish them for breaking those Lawes which he himself had necessitated them to break, which it was no more in their power not to break, then it is in the power of the fire not to burn? Excuse me if I hate this doctrine with a perfect hatred, which is so dishonorable both to God and man, which makes men to blaspheme of necessity, to steal of necessity, to be hanged of necessity, and to be damned of necessity. And therefore I must say and say again; *Quicquid ostendes mihi sic incredulis odi.* It were better to be an Atheist, to believe no God; or to be a Manichee, to believe two Gods, a God of good, and a God of evill; or with the Heathens, to believe thirty thousand Gods, than thus to charge the true God to be the proper cause and the true Author of all the sins and evills which are in the world.

J. D.

J. D.

Numb. 12.
Arg. 5.

Firstly, if there be no liberty, there shall be no day of Doom, no last Judgment, no rewards nor punishments after death. A man can never make himself a criminall, if he be not left at liberty to commit a crime. No man can be justly punished for doing that, which was not in his power to shun. To take away liberty, hazards heaven, but undoubtedly it leaves no hell.

T. H.

THE Arguments of greatest consequence are the third and fift, and fall both into one. Namely, If there be a necessity of all events, that it will follow, that praise and reprehension, reward and punishment, are all vain and unjust. And that if God should openly forbid, and secretly necessitate the same action, punishing men for what they could not avoid, there would be no belief among them of heaven or hell.

To oppose hereunto, I must borrow an answer from St. Paul, Rom. 9. ver. 11. *from the* 11. *verse of the Chapter to the* 18. *is laid down the very same objection in these words. When they (meaning* Esau *and* Jacob) *were yet unborn, and had done neither good nor evill, That the purpose of God according to election, not by works, but by him that calleth, might remain firm, it was said to her (viz. to* Rebekah) *that the elder shall serve the younger. And what then shall we say, is there injustice with God? God forbid. It is not therefore in him that willeth, nor in him that runneth, but in God that sheweth mercy. For the Scripture saith*

saith to Pharaoh, *I have stirred thee up, that I may shew my power in thee, and that my Name may be set forth in all the earth.* Therefore whom God willeth, he hath mercy on, and whom he willeth he hardeneth. Thus you see the case put by St. Paul is the same with that of J. D. and the same objection in these words following, *Thou wilt ask me then, why will God yet complain, for who hath resisted his will?* To this therefore the *Apostle* answers, not by denying it was Gods will, or that the decree of God concerning Esau *was not before he had sinned*, or that Esau *was not necessitated to do what he did*, but thus, *Who art thou, O Man, that interrogatest God? shall the work say to the workman, why hast thou made me thus? Hath not the Potter power over the clay of the same stuff, to make one vessell to honour, another to dishonour?* According therefore to this answer of St. Paul, I answer J. D's objection, and say The power of God alone, without other help, is sufficient Justification of any action he doth. That which men make among themselves here by pacts and Covenants, and call by the name of Justice and according whereunto men are counted and tearmed rightly just and unjust, is not that by which God Almighties actions are to be measured or called just, no more than his counsailes are to be measured by human wisedom. That which he does is made just by his doing; Just I say in him, not always just in us by the Examples; for a man that shall command a thing openly, and plot secretly the hinderance of the same, if he punish him, he so commanded for not doing it is unjust,

just. So also his counsailes, they be therefore not in vain, because they be his, whether we see the use of them or not. When God afflicted Job, he did object no sin to him, but justified that afflicting him by telling him of his power. Hast thou (sayes God) an arm like mine? Where wast thou when I layd the foundations of the earth? and the like. So our Saviour concerning the man that was born blind, said, it was not for his sin, nor his parents sin, but that the power of God might be shewn in him. Beasts are subject to death and torment, yet they cannot sin. It was Gods will it should be so. Power irresistible justifieth all actions really and properly in whomsoever it be found. Less power does not. And because such power is in God only, he must needs be just in all his actions. And we, that not comprehending his Counsailes, call him to the Bar, commit injustice in it.

I am not ignorant of the usuall reply to this answer by distinguishing between will and permission. As, that God Almighty does indeed permit sin sometimes, And that he also foreknoweth that the sin he permitteth shall be committed, but does not will it, nor necessitate it. I know also they distinguish the action from the sin of the action, saying, God Almighty does indeed cause the action, whatsoever action it be, but not the sinfulness or irregularity of it, that is, the discordance between the Action and the Law. Such distinctions as these dazell my understanding. I find no difference between the will to have a thing done, and the permission to do it, when he that permitteth it can hinder it, and knowes it will be

done

done *unless he hinder it. Nor find I any difference between an action that is against the Law, and the sin of that action. As for example, between the killing of* Uriah, *and the sin of* David *in killing* Uriah. *Nor when one is cause both of the action and of the Law, how another can be cause of the disagreement between them, no more than how one man making a longer and shorter garment, another can make the inequallity that is between them. This I know, God cannot sin, because his doing a thing makes it just, and consequenly no sin. And because whatsoever can sin, is subject to anothers Law, which God is not. And therefore tis blasphemy to say, God can sin. But to say, that God can so order the world as a sin may be necessarily caused thereby in a man, I do not see how it is any dishonour to him. Howsoever, if such or other distinctions can make it clear that* St. Paul *did not think* Esaus *or* Pharaohs *actions proceed from the will and purpose of God, or that proceeding from his will could not therefore without injustice be blamed or punished, I will as soon as I understand them turn unto* J. D's *opinion. For I now hold nothing in all this question between us, but what seemeth to me not obscurely, but most expresly said in this place by* Saint Paul. *And thus much in answer to his places of Scripture.*

J. D.

J. D.

T. H. thinks to kill two birds with one stone and satisfies two Arguments with one answer whereas in truth he satisfieth neither. First, for my third reason. Though all he say here, were as true as an Oracle. Though punishment were an act of dominion, not of Justice in God; yet this is no sufficient cause why God should deny his own Act, or why he should chide or expostulate with men, why they did that which he himself did necessitate them to do, and whereof he was the actor more than they, they being but as the stone, but he the hand that threw it. Notwithstanding any thing which is pleaded here, this Stoicall opinion doth stick hypocrisy and dissimulation close to God, who is the Truth it self.

And to my fift Argument, which he chargeth and relateth amiss, as by comparing mine with his, may appear. His chiefest answer is to oppose a difficult place of *St. Paul, Rom.* 9. 11. Hath he never heard, that to propose a doubt is not to answer an Argument, *Nec bene respondet qui litem lite resolvit*. But I will not pay him in his own coin. Wherefore to this place alledged by him, I answer, The case is not the same. The question moved there, is, how God did keep his promise made to Abraham *to be the God of him and of his seed*, if the Jewes who were the legitimate progeny of *Abraham* were deserted. To which the Apostle answers ver. 6. 7, 8. That that promise was not made to the carnall seed of *Abraham*, that is, the Jewes, but to his spirituall

tuall Sons which were the Heirs of his Faith, that is to the beleeving Christians; which answer he explicateth, first by the Allegory of *Isaack* and *Ishmael*, and after in the place cited of *Esau* and of *Jacob*. Yet neither doth he speak there so much of their persons as of their posterities. And though some words may be accommodated to Gods prædestination, which are there uttered, yet it is not the scope of that text, to treat of the reprobation of any man to hell-fire. All the posterity of *Esau* were not eternally reprobated, as holy *Job* and many others. But this question which is now agitated between us, is quite of another nature, how a man can be a criminal who doth nothing but that which he is extrinsecally necessitated to do, or how God in Justice can punish a man with æternall torments, for doing that, which it was never in his power to leave undone. That he who did impresite the motion in the heart of man, should punish man, who did onely receive the impression from him. So his answer looks *another way*.

But because he grounds so much upon this text, that if it can be cleared he is ready to change his opinion, I will examin all those passages which may seem to favour his cause. First, these words ver. 11. *being not yet borne, neither having done any good or evill,* upon which the whole weight of his argument doth depend, have no reference at all to those words ver. 13. Jacob *have I loved, and* Esau *have I hated,* for those words were first uttered by the

F 2 Prophet

Prophet *Malachy*, many ages after *Jacob* and *Esau* were dead, *Mal.* 1. 2. and intended of the posterity of *Esau*, who were not redeemed from captivity, as the *Israelites* were. But they are referred to those other words, ver. 12. *The elder shall serve the younger*, which indeed were spoken before *Jacob* or *Esau* were Born, *Gen.* 5. 23. And though those words of *Malachy* had been used of *Jacob* and *Esau* before they were Born, yet it had advantaged his cause nothing, for hatred in that text doth not signify any reprobation to the flames of hell, much less the execution of that decree, or the actuall imposition of punishment, nor any act contrary to love. God saw all that he made, and it was very good. Goodness it self cannot hate that which is good. But hatred there signifies Comparative hatred, or a less degree of love, or at the most a negation of love. As *Gen.* 29. 31. *When the Lord saw that Leah was hated*, we may not conclude thence that *Jacob* hated his Wife, The precedent verse doth fully expound the sense, ver. 30. Jacob *loved* Rachel *more then* Leah. So *Mat.* 6. 24. No man can serve two Masters, for either he will hate the one and love the other. So *Luke* 14. 26. If any Man hate not his Father and Mother, &c. he cannot be my Disciple. St. *Mathew* tells us the sense of it *Math.* 10. 37. *He that loveth Father or Mother more then me, is not worthy of me.*

Secondly, those words ver. 15. *I will have mercy on whom I will have mercy*, do prove
ne

no more but this, that the preferring of *Jacob* before *Esau*, and of the Christians before the Jews, was not à debt from God, either to the one or to the other, but a work of mercy. And what of this? All men confess that Gods mercies do exceed mans deserts, but Gods punishments do never exceed mans misdeeds. As we see in the Parable of the Labourers, *Matth.* 20. *Friend, I do thee no wrong, did not I agree with thee for a penny, Is it not lawfull for me to do with mine own as I will? Is thy eye evill because I am good?* Acts of Mercy are free, but acts of Justice are due.

That which follows ver. 17. comes something nearer the cause, *The Scripture saith unto* Pharoah, *for this same purpose I have raised thee up*, (that is, I have made thee a King, or I have preserved thee) *that I might shew my power in thee.* But this particle (that) doth not alwaies signifie the main end of an action, but sometimes onely a consequent of it. As *Matth.* 2. 15. He departed into *Egypt*, that it might be fulfilled which was spoken by the Prophet, out of *Egypt* have I called my Son; without doubt *Josephs* aim or end of his journey was not to fulfill prophesies, but to save the life of the Child. Yet because the fulfilling of the prophecy was a consequent of *Josephs* journy, he saith, *That it might be fulfilled.* So here, *I have raised thee up that I might shew my power.* Again, though it should be granted that this particle, *that*, did denote the intention of God to destroy *Pharaoh* in the Red Sea, yet it was not the Antecedent intention of God, which evermore respects the good and benefit of the creature, but Gods consequent intention upon the prævision of *Pharaohs* obstinacy, that since he would not glorifie God in obeying his word, he should glorifie God undergoing his judgements, Hitherto we find no æternal punishments nor no temporal punishment without just deserts.

It follows ver. 18. *whom he will he hardneth*: Indeed hardness of heart is the greatest judgement that Gods lays upon a sinner in this life, worse then all the Plagues of *Egypt*. But how doth God harden the heart? not by a naturall influence of any evill act or habit into the will, nor by inducing the will with perswasive motives to obstinacy and rebellion, *for God tempteth no man, but every man is tempted when he is drawn away of his own lust and intised.* Jam. 1.13. Then God is said to harden

1. the heart three wayes, First, negatively, and not positively, not by imparting wickedness, but by not imparting grace, as the Sun descending to the tropick of *Capricorne*, it is said with us to be the cause of Winter, that is, not by imparting cold, but by not imparting heat. It is an act of mercy in God to give his grace freely, but to detein it is no act of injustice. So the Apostle opposeth hardning to shewing of mercy, To harden is as much as not to shew mercy.

2. Secondly, God is said to harden the heart occasionally and not causally, by doing good, which incorrigible sinners make an occasion of growing worse and worse, and doing evill; as a

Master

Master by often correcting of an untoward Scholar, doth accidentally and occasionally harden his heart, and render him more obdurate, insomuch as he growes even to despise the Rod. Or as an indulgent parent by his patience and gentlenefs doth incourage an obstinate son to become more rebellious. So, whether we look upon Gods frequent judgments upon *Pharaoh*, or Gods iterated favours in removing and withdrawing those judgments upon *Pharaohs* request, both of them in their severall kinds, were occasions of hardning *Pharaohs* heart, the one making him more presumptuous, the other more desperately rebellious. So that which was good, in it was Gods; that which was evill was *Pharaohs*. God gave the occasion, but *Pharaoh* was the true cause of his own obduration. This is cleerly confirmed Gen. 8. 15. *When* Pharaoh *saw that thers was respite, he hardned his heart.* And Gen. 9. 34. *When* Pharaoh *saw, that the Rain and the Hail, and the Thunders were ceased, he sinned yet more, and hardned his heart, he and his servants.* So Psal. 105. 25. *He turned their hearts, so that they hated his people, and dealt subtilly with them:* That is, God blessed the Children of *Israel*, whereupon the *Egyptians* did take occasion to hate them, as is plain *Exod.* 1. ver. 7, 8, 9, 10. So God hardened *Pharaohs* heart, and *Pharaoh* hardened his own heart. God hardened it by not shewing mercy to *Pharaoh*, as he did to *Nebuchadnezzar*, who was as great a sinner as he, or God hardned it occasionally, but still *Pharaoh* was the true cause of his own obduration,

obduration, by determining his own will to evill, and confirming himself in his obstinacy. So are all presumptuous sinners Psal. 95. 8. *Harden not your hearts as in the provocation, as in the day of temptation in the wildernefs.*

3   Thirdly, God is said to harden the heart permissively, but not operatively, nor effectively, as he who only lets loose a Greyhound out of the slip, is said to hound him at the Hare. Will you see plainly what St. *Paul* intends by hardning? Read ver. 22. *What if God willing to shew his wrath and to make his power known* (that is, by a consequent will, which in order of nature followes the provision of sin,) *indured with much long suffering the vessells of wrath fitted to destruction. And that he might make known the riches of his glory on the vessells of mercy, &c.* There is much difference between *induring* and *impelling*, or inciting the vessells of wrath. He saith of the vessells of mercy, that *God prepared them unto glory*. But of the vessells of wrath, he saith only, that they were *fitted to destruction*, that is, not by God, but by themselves. St. *Paul* faith, that God doth *endure the vessells of wrath with much long suffering*, T. H. saith, that God wills and effects by the second causes all their actions good and bad, that he necessitateth them, and determineth them irresistibly to do those acts which he condemneth as evill, and for which he punisheth them. *If doing willingly, and enduring, If much long suffering,* and *necessitating,* imply not a contrariety one to another, *reddat mihi minam Diogenes,* Let him that taught

me

me Logick, give me my money again.

But *T. H.* faith, that this diſtinction between the *operative* and *permiſſive* Will of God; And that other between the *action* and the irregularity do dazell his underſtanding. Though he can find no difference between theſe two, yet others do, *St. Paul* himſelf did, *Act.* 13. 18. *About the time of* 40. *yeares ſuffered he their manners in the Wilderneſs.* And *Act.* 14. 16. *Who in times paſt ſuffered all Nations to walk in their own wayes.* T. H. would make ſuffering to be inciting, their manners to be Gods manners, their wayes to be Gods wayes. And *Act.* 17. 30. *The times of this ignorance God winked at.* It was never heard that one was ſaid to wink or connive at that which was his own act. And 1 *Cor.* 10. 13. *God is faithfull, who will not ſuffer you to be tempted above that you are able.* To tempt is the Devills act, therefore he is called the *Tempter*, God tempts no man to ſin, but he ſuffers them to be tempted. And ſo ſuffers, that he could hinder Sathan, if he would. But by *T. H.* his doctrine, To tempt to ſin, and to ſuffer one to be tempted to ſin, when it is in his power to hinder it, is all one. And ſo he transforms God (I write it with horrour) into the Devill, and makes tempting to be Gods own work, and the Devill to be but his inſtrument. And in that noted place, *Rom.* 2. 4. *Deſpiſeſt thou the riches of his goodneſs, and forbearance, and long-ſuffering, not knowing that the goodneſs of God leadeth thee to repentance, but after thy hardneſs and impenitent heart treaſureſt up unto thy ſelf wrath againſt the day of wrath,*

wrath, and revealation of the righteous judgment of God. Here are as many convincing Arguments in this one text against the opinion of *T. H.* almost as there are words. Here we learn that God is *rich in goodness*, and will not punish his creatures for that which is his own act; Secondly, that he *suffers* and *forbeares sinners long*, and doth not snatch them away by sudden death as they deserve. Thirdly, that the reason of Gods forbearance is to *bring men to repentance*. Fourthly, that *hardness of heart and impenitency* is not casually from God, but from our selves. Fiftly, that it is not the insufficient proposall of the means of their conversion on Gods part, which is the cause of mens perdition, but their own contempt and *despising* of these means. Sixtly, that punishment is not an act of absolute dominion, but an act of *righteous Judgment*, whereby God renders to every man according to his own deeds, wrath to them and only to them who *treasure up wrath unto themselves*, and eternall life to those *who continue patiently in well-doing*. If they deserve such punishment who onely neglect the goodness and long suffering of God, what do they who utterly deny it, and make Gods doing and his suffering to be all one? I do beseech *T. H.* to consider what a degree of wilfulness it is, out of one obscure text wholly misunderstood, to contradict the clear current of the whole Scripture. Of the same mind with St. *Paul* was St. *Peter*, 1 Pet. 3. 22. *The long suffering of God waited once in the dayes of Noah.* And 2 Pet. 3. 15. *Account that the long suffering of the Lord is salvation.* This
is

is the name God gives himself. Exod. 34. 6. *The Lord, the Lord God, mercifull and gracious, long suffering, &c.*

Yet I do acknowledge that which *T. H.* saith to be commonly true, That he who doth permit any thing to be done, which it is in his power to hinder, knowing that if he do not hinder it, it will be done, doth in some sort will it. I say in some sort, that is, either by an antecedent will, or by a consequent will, either by an operative will, or by a permissive will, or he is willing to let it be done, but not willing to do it. Sometimes an antecedent engagement doth cause a man to suffer that to be done, which otherwise he would not suffer. So *Darius* suffered *Daniel* to be cast into the Lions den, to make good his rash decree; So *Herod* suffered *John Baptist* to be beheaded, to make good his rash oath; How much more may the immutable rule of justice in God, and his fidelity in keeping his word, draw from him the punishment of obstinate sinners, though antecedently he willeth their conversion? He loveth all his Creatures well, but his own Justice better. Again, sometimes a man suffereth that to be done, which he doth not will directly in it self, but indirectly for some other end, or for the producing of some great good; As a man willeth that a putrid member be cut off from his body, to save the life of the whole. Or as a Judge being desirous to save a malefactors life, and having power to repreive him, doth yet condemn him for example sake, that by the death of one, he may
save

save the lives of many. Marvell not then if God suffer some creatures to take such courses as tend to their own ruine, so long as their sufferings do make for the greater manifestation of his glory, and for the greater benefit of his faithfull servants. This is a most certain truth, that God would not suffer evill to be in the world, unless he knew how to draw good out of evill. Yet this ought not to be so understood, as if we made any priority or posteriority of time in the acts of God, but onely of nature. Nor do we make the antecedent and consequent will to be contrary one to another, because the one respects man pure and uncorrupted, the other respects him as he is lapsed. The objects are the same, but considered after a diverse manner. Nor yet do we make these wills to be distinct in God, for they are the same with the divine essence, which is one. But the distinction is in order to the objects or things willed. Nor, lastly, do we make this permission to be a naked or a meer permission, God causeth all good, permitteth all evill, disposeth all things, both good and evill.

T. H. demands how God should be the cause of the action and yet not be the cause of the irregularity of the action. I answer, because he concurres to the doing of evill by a generall, but not by a speciall influence. As the Earth gives nourishment to all kinds of plants, as well to Hemlock as to Wheat, but the reason why the one yields food to our sustenance, the other poison to our destruction, is not from the generall nourishment of the earth, but from the

speciall

speciall quality of the root. Even so the generall power to act is from God, *In him we live, and move, and have our being*. This is good. But the specification, and determination, of this generall power, to the doing of any evill, is from our selves, and proceeds from the free will of man; This is bad. And to speak properly, the free will of man is not the efficient cause of sin, as the root of the Hemlock is of poison, sin having no fruentity or being in it, as poison hath. But rather the deficient cause. Now no defect can flow from him who is the highest perfection. Wherefore *T. H.* is mightily mistaken, to make the particular and determinate act of killing *Uriah* to be from God. The generall power to act is from God, but the specification of this generall and good power to murther, or to any particular evill, is not from God, but from the free will of man. So *T. H.* may see clearly if he will, how one may be the cause of the Law, and likewise of the action in some sort, that is, by generall influence; and yet another cause concurring by speciall influence and determining this generall and good power may make it self the true cause of the anomy or the irregularity. And therefore he may keep his longer and shorter garments for some other occasion. Certainly, they will not fit this subject, unless he could make generall and speciall influence to be all one.

But *T. H.* presseth yet further, that the case is the same, and the objection used by the Jews, ver. 19. *Why doth he yet find fault? who hath resisted*

sisted his will? is the very same with my argument; And *St. Pauls* answer ver. 20. *O man who art thou that repliest against God? shall the thing formed say to him that formed it, why hast thou made me thus? Hath not the Potter power over his clay, &c?* is the very same with his answer in this place, drawn from the irresistible power, and absolute dominion of God, which justifieth all his actions. And that the Apostle in his answer doth not deny, that it was Gods will, nor that Gods decree was before *Esau* sin. To which I reply.

First, that the case is not at all the same, but quite different, as may appear by these particulars; first, those words, *before they had done either good or evill*, are not, cannot be referred to those other words, *Esau have I hated*; Secondly, If they could, yet it is less than nothing, because before *Esau* had actually sinned, his future sins were known to God; Thirdly, by the Potters clay, here is not to be understood the pure mass, but the corrupted mass of mankind. Fourthly, the hating here mentioned is onely a comparative hatred, that is, a less degree of love. Fiftly, the hardening which *St. Paul* speaks of, is not a positive, but a negative obduration, or a not imparting of grace. Sixtly, St. *Paul* speaketh not of any positive reprobation to eternall punishment, much less doth he speak of the actuall inflicting of punishment without sin, which is the question between us, and wherein *T. H.* differs from all that I remember to have read, who do all acknowledge that punishment is never actually inflicted but for sin. If the question be put, why God doth good to one more than to another, or why God imparteth more grace to one than to another, as it is there, the answer is just and fit, because it is his pleasure, and it is sawciness in a creature in this case to reply, *May not God do what he will with his own*, Matth. 20. 15. No man doubteth but God imparteth grace beyond mans desert; But if the case be put, why God doth punish one more than another, or why he throws one into hell-fire, and not another, which is the present case agitated between us; To say with *T. H.* that it is because God is Omnipotent, or because his power is irresistible, or meerly because it is his pleasure, is not only not warranted, but is plainly condemned by St. *Paul* in this place. So many differences there are between those two cases. It is not therefore against God, that I reply, but against *T. H.* I do not call my Creator to the Bar, but my fellow creature; I ask no account of Gods counsails, but of mans presumptions. It is the mode of these times to father their own fancies upon God, and when they cannot justifie them by reason, to plead his Omnipotence, or to cry, *O altitudo*, that the wayes of God are unsearchable. If they may justifie their drowsy dreams, because Gods power & dominion is absolute; much more may we reject such phantasticall devises which are inconsistent with the truth, and goodness &, Justice of God, and make him to be a Tyrant, who is the Father of Mercies, and the God of all consolation

tion. The unsearchableness of Gods wayes should be a bridle to restrain presumption, and not a sanctuary for spirits of error.

2   Secondly, this objection conteined ver. 19. to which the Apostle answers ver. 20. is not made in the person of *Esau* or *Pharaoh*, as *T.H.* supposeth, but of the unbelieving Jews, who thought much at that grace and favour which God was pleased to vouchsafe unto the Gentiles, to acknowledge them for his people, which honour they would have appropriated to the posterity of *Abraham*. And the Apostles answer is not only drawn from the Soveraign Dominion of God, to impart his grace to whom he pleaseth, as hath been shewed already, but also from the obstinacy and proper fault of the Jews, as appeareth ver. 22. *What if God willing* (that is, by a consequent will) *to shew his wrath, and to make his power known, endured with much long suffering the vessels of wrath fitted to destruction.* They acted, God endured; They were tolerated by God, but fitted to destruction by themselves, for their much wrong doing, here is Gods *much long suffering*; And more plainly ver. 31. *Israel hath not atteined to the Law of righteousness, wherefore? because they sought it not by faith, but as it were by the works of the Law.* This reason is set down yet more emphatically in the next Chapter ver. 3. *They* (that is, *the Israelites*) *being ignorant of Gods righteousness* (that is, by faith in Christ,) *and going about to establish their own righteousness,* (that is, by the works of the Law) *have not submitted them-*
selves

selves to the righteousness of God. And yet most expresly Chap. 11. v. 20. *Because of unbelief they were broken off, but thou standest by faith,* Neither was there any precedent binding decree of God, to necessitate them to unbelief, and consequently to punishment. It was in their own power by their concurrence with Gods grace to prevent these judgments, and to recover their former estate, ver. 23. *If they* (that is, the unbelieving Jews) *abide not still in unbelief, they shall be graffed in.* The Crown and the Sword are immovable, (to use St. *Anselmes* comparison) but it is we that move and change places. Sometimes the Jews were under the Crown, and the Gentiles under the Sword, sometimes the Jews under the Sword, and the Gentiles under the Crown.

Thirdly, though I confess, that human Pacts are not the measure of Gods Justice, but his justice is his own immutable will, whereby he is ready to give every man that which is his own: as rewards to the good, punishments to the bad, so nevertheless God may oblige himself freely to his creature. He made the Covenant of works with mankind in *Adam*, and therefore he punisheth not man contrary to his own Covenant, but for the transgression of his duty. And Divine Justice is not measured by Omnipotence, or by irresistible power, but by Gods will; God can do many things according to his absolute power which he doth not; He could raise up children to *Abraham* of stones, but he never did so. It is a rule in Theology, that God cannot do any thing which argues any wickedness or imperfeperfection, as God cannot deny himself, 2 *Tim.* 2. 13. He cannot lie, *Tit.* 1. 2. These and the like are fruits of impotence, not of power. So God cannot destroy the righteous with the wicked, *Gen.* 18. 25. He could not destroy *Sodome* whilst *Lot* was in it, *Gen.* 19. 22. not for want of dominion or power, but because it was not agreeable to his Justice, nor to that Law which himself had constituted. The Apostle saith Heb. 6. 10. *God is not unrighteous to forget your work.* As it is a good consequence to say, this is from God, therefore it is righteous, so is this also; This thing is unrighteous, therefore it cannot proceed from God. We see how all Creatures by instinct of nature do love their young, as the Hen her Chickens, how they will expose themselves to death for them; And yet all these are but shadowes of that love which is in God towards his Creatures. How impious is it then to conceive, that God did creat so many millions of souls to be tormented eternally in hell, without any fault of theirs, except such as he himself did necessitate them unto, meerly to shew his dominion, and because his power is irresistible? The same privilege which *T. H.* appropriates here to power absolutely irresistible, a friend of his in his book *de Cive cap. 6. pag.* 70. ascribes to power respectively irresistible, or to Soveraign Magistrates, whose power he makes to be as absolute as a mans power is over himself, not to be limitted by any thing, but only by their strength. The greatest propugners of Soveraign power think it enough for Princes to challenge an immunity

from

from coercive power, but acknowledge, that the Law hath a directive power over them. But *T. H.* will have no limits but their strength. Whatsoever they do by power, they do justly.

But, saith he, God objected no sin to *Job*, but justified his afflicting him by his power. First, this is an Argument from authority negatively, that is to say, worth nothing. Secondly, the afflictions of *Job* were no vindicatory punishments to take vengeance of his sins, (whereof we dispute,) but probatory chastisements to make triall of his graces. Thirdly, *Job* was not so pure, but that God might justly have laid greater punishments upon him, then those afflictions which he suffered. Witness his impatience, even to the cursing of the day of his nativity, *Job* 3. 3. Indeed God said to *Job*, *where wast thou when I laid the foundations of the earth?* Job 38. 4. that is, how canst thou judge of the things that were done before thou wast born? or comprehend the secret causes of my judgments? And Job 42. 9. *Hast thou an arm like God?* As if he should say, why art thou impatient? doest thou think thy self able to strive with God? But that God should punish *Job* without desert, here is not a word.

Concerning the blind man, mentioned *John* 9. his blindness was rather a blessing to him than a punishment, being the means to raise his Soul illuminated, and to bring him to see the face of God in Jesus Christ. The sight of the body is common to us with Ants and Flies, but the sight of the soul with the blessed Angells. We read of some, who have put out their bodily eyes because they thought they were an impediment to the eye of the Soul. Again, neither he nor his parents were innocent, being conceived and born in sin and iniquity, *Psal.* 51. 5. And in many things we offend all, *Jam.* 3. 2. But our Saviours meaning is evident by the Disciples question, ver. 2. They had not so sinned, that he should be born blind. Or they were not more grievous sinners than other men, to deserve an exemplary judgment more than they; but this corporall blindness befell him principally by the extraordinary providence of God, for the manifestation of his own glory, in restoring him to his sight. So his instance halts on both sides; neither was this a punishment, nor the blind man free from sin. His third instance of the death and torments of beasts, is of no more weight then the two former. The death of brute beasts is not a punishment of sin, but a debt of nature. And though they be often slaughtered for the use of man, yet there is a vast difference between those light and momentary pangs, and the unsufferable and endless pains of hell; between the meer depriving of a creature of temporall life, and the subjecting of it to eternall death; I know the Philosophicall speculations of some who affirme, that entity is better than non-entity, that it is better to be miserable, and suffer the torments of the damned, than to be annihilated, and cease to be altogether. This entity which they speak of, is a Metaphysicall entity abstracted from the matter, which is better

than

than non-entity, in respect of some goodness, not morall nor naturall, but transcendentall, which accompanies every being. But in the concrete it is far otherwise, where that of our Saviour often takes place, Matth. 26. 24. *Woe unto that man by whom the Son of Man is betrayed, It had been good for that man, that he had not been born.* I add, that there is an Analogicall Justice and Mercy due, even to the brute beasts. *Thou shalt not muffle the mouth of the Oxe that treadeth out the corn.* And, *a just man is mercifull to his beast.*

But his greatest errour is that which I touched before, to make Justice to be the proper result of Power. Power doth not measure and regulate Justice, but Justice measures & regulates Power. The will of God, and the Eternall Law which is in God himself, is properly the rule and measure of Justice. As all goodness whether Naturall or Morall, is a participation of divine goodness, and all created Rectitude is but a participation of divine rectitude, so all Lawes are but participations of the eternall Law, from whence they derive their power. The rule of Justice then is the same both in God and us, but it is in God, as in him that doth regulate and measure; in us, as in those who are regulated and measured. As the will of God is immutable, alwayes willing what is just and right and good; So his justice likewise is immutable. And that individuall action which is justly punished as sinfull in us, cannot possibly proceed from the speciall influence and determinative power of a

just

just cause. See then how grossely *T. H.* doth understand that old and true principle, that *the Will of God is the rule of Justice*, as if by willing things in themselves unjust, he did render them just, by reason of his absolute dominion and irresistible power. As fire doth assimilate other things to it self, and convert them into the nature of fire. This were to make the eternall Law a *Lesbian* rule. Sin is defined to be *that which is done, or said, or thought contrary to the eternall Law*. But by this doctrine nothing is done, nor said, nor thought contrary to the will of God. St. *Anselm* said most truly, *then the will of man is good and just and right, when he wills that which God would have him to will*: but according to this doctrine every man alwayes wills that which God would have him to will. If this be true, we need not pray, *Thy will be done in earth as it is in heaven*, *T. H.* hath devised a new kind of heaven upon earth. The worst is, it is an heaven without Justice. Justice is a constant and perpetuall act of the will, to give every one his own; But to inflict punishment for those things which the Judge himself did determine and necessitate to be done, is not to give every one his own; right punitive Justice is a relation of equallity and proportion, between the demerit and the punishment; But supposing this opinion of absolute and universall necessity, there is no demerit in the world, we use to say, that right springs from Law and fact, as in this Syllogism, Every thief ought to be punished, there's the Law; But such an one is a thief,
there's

there's the fact, therefore he ought to be punished, there's the right. But this opinion of *T. H.* grounds the right to be punished, neither upon Law, nor upon Fact, but upon the irresistible power of God. Yea, it overturneth as much, as in it lies all Law; First, the eternall Law, which is the ordination of divine Wisdom, by which all Creatures are directed to that end which is convenient for them. That is, not to necessitate them to eternall flames. Then, the Law, participated, which is the ordination of right reason, instituted for the common good, to shew unto man, what he ought to do, and what he ought not to do. To what purpose is it to shew the right way to him who is drawn and haled a contrary way by Adamantine bonds of inevitable necessity?

Lastly, howsoever *T. H.* cries out, that God cannot sin, yet in truth he makes him to be the principall and most proper cause of all sin. For, he makes him to be the cause not onely of the Law, and of the action, but even of the irregularity it self, and the difference between the action and the Law, wherein the very essence of sin doth consist. He makes God to determin *Davids* will, and necessitate him to kill *Uriah*. In causes physically, and essentially subordinate, the cause of the cause is evermore the cause of the effect. These are those deadly fruits which spring from the poisonous root of the absolute necessity of all things, which *T. H.* seeing, and that neither the sins of *Esau*, nor *Pharaoh*, nor any wicked person do proceed from the operative,

tive, but from the permissive will of God; And that punishment is an act of justice, not of dominion onely, I hope that according to his promise he will change his opinion.

J. D.

Proofs of Liberty drawn from reason.

Arg. 9.
Numb. 13.

THe first argument is *Herculeum* or *Baculinum*, drawn from that pleasant passage between *Zeno* and his man; The servant had committed some pettilarceny, and the master was cudgelling him well for it; The servant thinks to creep under his masters blind-side, and pleades for himself; That *the necessity of destiny did compell him to steal*. The master answers, *the same necessity of destiny compells me to beat thee*. He that denies liberty is fitter to be refuted with rodds, than with arguments, untill he confess that it is free for him that beates him either to continue striking, or to give over, that is, to have true liberty.

T. H.

OF the *Arguments from reason, the first is, that which he saith, is drawn from* Zenos *beating of his man which is therefore called* Argumentum baculinum, *that is to say, a wooden Argument. The story is this,* Zeno *held that all actions were necessary, His man therefore being for some fault beaten, excused himself upon the necessity of it. To avoid this excuse, his master pleaded likewise the necessity of beating him. So that not he that mainteined, but he that derided the necessity of things was beaten, contrary to that he would infer; And the argument was rather withdrawn than drawn from the story.*

J. D.

Whether the argument be withdrawn from the story, or the answer withdrawn from the argument, let the Reader judge. *T. H.* mistakes the scope of the reason, the strength whereof doth not lie, neither in the authority of *Zeno*, a rigid Stoick, which is not worth a button in this cause; Nor in the servants being an adversary to Stoicall necessity, for it appeares not out of the story, that the servant did deride necessity, but rather that he pleaded it in good earnest for his own justification. Now in the successe of the fray, we were told even now, that no power doth justifie an action, but onely that which is irresistible. Such was not *Zenos*. And therefore it advantageth neither of their causes, neither that of *Zeno*, nor this of *T. H.* What if the servant had taken the staff out of his masters hand and beaten him soundly, would not the same argument have served the man as well as it did the master? that the necessity of destiny did compell him to strike again. Had not *Zeno* smarted justly for his Paradox? And might not the spectators well have taken up the Judges Apothegm, concerning the dispute between *Corax* and his Schollar, *An ill egg of an ill bird*? But the strength of this argument lies partly in the ignorance of *Zeno*, that great Champion of necessity, and the beggarlinesse of his cause, which admitted no defence but with a cudgell. No man (saith the servant) ought to be beaten for

for doing that which he is compelled inevitably to do, but I am compelled inevitably to steal. The major is so evident, that it cannot be denied. If a strong man shall take a weak mans hand perforce, and do violence with it to a third person, he whose hand is forced, is innocent, and he only culpable who compelled him. The minor was *Zenos* own doctrine; what answer made the great patron of destiny to his servant? very learnedly he denied the conclusion, and cudgelled his servant, telling him in effect, that though there was no reason why he should be beaten, yet there was a necessity why he must be beaten. And partly, in the evident absurdity of such an opinion which deserves not to be confuted with reasons, but with rods. There are four things, said the Philosoher, which ought not to be called into question, First, such things whereof it is wickedness to doubt; as whether the soul be immortall, whether there be a God, such an one should not be confuted with reasons, but cast into the sea, with a millstone about his neck, as unworthy to breath the aire, or to behold the light. Secondly, such things as are above the capacity of reason; as among Christians, the mystery of the holy Trinity. Thirdly, such principles as are evidently true; as that two and two are foure in Arithmetick, that the whole is greater than the part in Logick. Fourthly, such things as are obvious to the senses; as whether the snow be white. He who denied the heat of the fire, was justly sentenced to be scorched with fire; and he that denied motion, to be beaten

untill

untill he recanted. So he who denies all liberty from necessitations, should be scourged untill he become an humble suppliant to him that whips him, and confess, that he hath power, either to strike, or to hold his hand.

J. D.

SEcondly, this very perswasion, that there is no true liberty is able to overthrow all Societies and Commonwealths in the world. The Lawes are unjust which prohibite that which a man cannot possibly shun; All consultations are vain, if every thing be either necessary or impossible. Who ever deliberated, whether the Sun should rise to morrow, or whether he should sail over mountains? It is to no more purpose to admonish men of understanding than fools, children, or madmen, if all things be necessary. Praises and dispraises, rewards and punishments are as vain as they are undeserved, if there be no liberty. All Councells, Arts, Arms, Books, Instruments, are superfluous and foolish, if there be no liberty; In vain we labour, in vain we study, in vain we take Physick, in vain we have Tutours to instruct us, if all things come to pass alike, whether we sleep or wake, whether we be idle or industrious, by unalterable necessity. But it is said, that though future events be certain, yet they are unknown to us. And therefore we prohibite, deliberate, admonish, praise, dispraise, reward, punish, study, labour, and use means. Alas, how should our not knowing of the event be a sufficient motive to us to use the means, so long as we believe the event is already certainly determi-

Numb. 14.
Arg. 2.

determined, and can no more be changed by all our endeavours, than we can stay the course of Heaven with our finger, or add a cubite to our stature? Suppose it be unknown, yet it is certain. We cannot hope to alter the course of things by our labours; Let the necessary causes do their work, we have no remedy but patience, and shrug up the shoulders. Either allow liberty, or destroy all Societies.

T. H.

THE second argument is taken from certain inconveniences which he thinks would follow such an opinion. It is true, that ill use may be made of it, and therefore your Lordship and J. D. *ought at my request to keep private, that I say here of it. But the inconveniences are indeed none; and what use soever be made of truth, yet truth is truth; and now the question is not what is fit to be preached, but what is true. The first inconvenience he sayes, is this, that Lawes which prohibite any action are then unjust. The second, that all consultations are vain. The third, that admonitions to men of understanding are of no more use than to fools, children and mad-men. The fourth, that praise, dispraise, reward and punishment are in vain. The fift, that Councells, Arts, Armes, Books, Instruments, Study, Tutours, Medicines are in vain. To which argument expecting I should answer by saying, that the ignorance of the event were enough to make us use means, he adds (as it were a reply to my answer foreseen) these words. Alas, how should our not knowing the event be a sufficient motive to make us use* the means? Wherein he saith right, but my answer is not that which he expecteth. I answer.

First, that the necessity of an action doth not make the Law which prohibits it unjust. To let pass, that not the necessity, but the will to break the Law maketh the action unjust, because the Law regardeth the will, and no other precedent causes of action. And to let pass, that no Law can be possibly unjust, in as much as every man makes by his consent the Law he is bound to keep, and which consequently must be just, unless a man can be unjust to himself; I say, what necessary cause soever preceds an action, yet if the action be forbidden, he that doth it willingly may justly be punisht. For instance, suppose the Law on pain of death prohibit stealing, and there be a man who by the strength of temptation is necessitated to steal, and is thereupon put to death, does not this punishment deterr others from theft? is it not a cause that others steal not? doth it not frame and make their will to justice? To make the Law is therefore to make a cause of Justice, and to necessitate justice, and consequently it is no injustice to make such a Law.

The institution of the Law is not to grieve the delinquent for that which is passed, and not to be undone, but to make him and others just, that els would not be so. And respecteth not the evill act past, but the good to come. In so much as without this good intention of future, no past Act of a delinquent could justifie his killing in the sight of God. But you will say, how is it just to

kill

kill one man to amend another, if what were done were necessary? To this I answer, that men are justly killed, not for that their actions are not necessitated, but that they are spared and preserved, because they are not noxious; for where there is no Law, there no killing, nor any thing els can be unjust. And by the right of Nature we destroy, without being unjust, all that is noxious, both beasts and men. And for beasts, we kill them justly, when we do it in order to our own preservation. And yet J. D. confesseth, that their actions, as being only spontaneous and not free, are all necessitated and determined to that one thing which they shall do. For men, when we make Societies or Commonwealths, we lay down our right to kill, excepting in certain cases, as murther, theft, or other offensive actions; So that the right which the Commonwealth hath to put a man to death for crimes, is not created by the Law, but remaines from the first right of nature, which every man hath to preserve himself, for that the Law doth not take that right away, in case of criminalls, who were by Law excepted. Men are not therefore put to death, or punished for that their theft proceedeth from election, but because it was noxious and contrary to mens preservation, and the punishment conducing to the preservation of the rest. In as much as to punish those that do voluntary hurt, and none els, frameth and maketh mens wills such as men would have them. And thus it is plain, that from necessity of a voluntary action cannot be inferred the injustice of the Law that forbiddeth it, or of the Magistrate that punisheth it.

Secondly,

Secondly, I deny that it makes consultations to be in vain; 'tis the consultation that causeth a man, and necessitateth him to choose to do one thing rather than another. So that unless a man say, that cause to be in vain, which necessitateth the effect, he cannot infer the superfluousness of consultation out of the necessity of the election proceeding from it. But it seemes he reasons thus, If I must needs do this rather than that, then I shall do this rather than that, though I consult not at all; which is a false proposition, a false consequence, and no better than this, If I shall live till to morrow, I shall live till to morrow, though I run my self through with a sword to day. If there be a necessity that an action shall be done, or that any effect shall be brought to pass, it does not therefore follow, that there is nothing necessarily required as a means to bring it to pass. And therefore when it is determined, that one thing shall be chosen before another, 'tis determined also for what cause it shall be chosen, which cause for the most part is deliberation or consultation. And therefore consultation is not in vain, and indeed the less in vain, by how much the election is more necessitated.

The same answer is to be given to the third supposed inconveniency; Namely, that admonitions are in vain, for admonitions are parts of consultations. The Admonitor being a Counsailer for the time, to him that is admonished.

The fourth pretended inconveniency is, that praise and dispraise, reward and punishment will be in vain. To which I answer, that for praise and

and dispraise, they depend not at all on the necessity of the action praised or dispraised. For, what is it els to praise, but to say a thing is good? Good, I say for me, or for some body els, or for the State and Commonwealth. And what is it to say an action is good, but to say, it is as I would wish, or as another would have it; or according to the will of the State, that is to say, according to Law? Does J. D. *think, that no action can please me or him, or the Commonwealth, that should proceed from necessity?*

Things may be therefore necessary, and yet prayseworthy, as also necessary, and yet dispraised, and neither of both in vain, because praise and dispraise, and likewise reward and punishment, do by example make and conform the will to good or evill. It was a very great praise in my opinion, that Velleius Paterculus *gives* Cato*, where he sayes, he was good by nature,* Et quia aliter esse non potuit.

The fift and sixt inconvenience, that Councells, Arts, Arms, Books, Instruments, Study, Medicines, and the like, would be superfluous, the same answer serves that to the former; That is to say, that this consequence, if the effect shall necessarily come to pass, then it shall come to pass without its cause, is a false one: And those things named, Councells, Arts, Arms, &c. are the causes of those effects.

J. D.

J. D.

NOthing is more familiar with *T. H.* than to decline an argument. But I will put it into form for him. The first inconvenience is thus pressed. Those Lawes are unjust and Tyrannicall, which do prescribe things absolutely impossible in themselves to be done, and punish men for not doing of them. But supposing *T. H.* his opinion of the necessity of all things to be true, all Lawes do prescribe absolute impossibilities to be done, and punish men for not doing of them. The former proposition is so clear, that it cannot be denied. Just Lawes are the Ordinances of right reason, but those Lawes which prescribe absolute impossibilities, are not the Ordinances of right reason. Just Lawes are instituted for the publick good, but those Lawes which prescribe absolute impossibilities are not instituted for the publick good. Just Laws do shew unto a man what is to be done, and what is to be shunned; But those Lawes which prescribe impossibilities, do not direct a man what he is to do, and what he is to shun. The Minor is as evident; for if his opinion be true all actions, all transgressions are determined antecedently inevitably to be done by a naturall and necessary flux of extrinsecall causes. Yea, even the will of man, and the reason it self is thus determined. And therefore whatsoever Laws do prescribe any thing to be done which is not done, or to be left undone which is done, do prescribe absolute impossibilities, and punish men for not doing of impossibilities. In all his

H answer

answer there is not one word to this argument, but only to the conclusion. He saith, that *not the necessity, but the will to break the Law makes the action unjust.* I ask what makes the will to break the Law, is it not his necessity? What getts he by this? A perverse will causeth injustice, and necessity causeth a perverse will. He saith, *the Law regardeth the will, but not the precedent causes of action.* To what proposition, to what tearm is this answer? he neither denies, nor distinguisheth. First, the question here is not what makes actions to be unjust, but what makes Lawes to be unjust. So his answer is impertinent. It is likewise untrue, for First, that will which the Law regards, is not such a will as *T. H.* imagineth. It is a free will, not a determined, necessitated will; a rationall will, not a brutish will. Secondly, the Law doth look upon precedent causes as well as the voluntarines of the action. If a child before he be seven years old, or have the use of reason, in some childish quarrell do willingly stab another, whereof we have seen experience, yet the Law looks not upon it as an act of murther, because there wanted a power to deliberate, and consequently true liberty. Man-slaughter may be as voluntary as murther, and commonly more voluntary, because being done in hot blood, there is the less reluctation, yet the Law considers, that the former is done out of some sudden passion without serious deliberation, and the other out of prepensed malice, and desire of revenge, and therefore condemnes murther as more wilfull

full and more punishable than man-slaughter.

He saith, *that no Law can possibly be unjust*; And I say, that this is to deny the conclusion, which deserves no reply; But to give him satisfaction, I will follow him in this also. If he intended no more, but that unjust Lawes are not Genuine Lawes, nor bind to active obedience, because they are not the ordinations of right reason, nor instituted for the common good, nor prescribe that which ought to be done, he said truly, but nothing at all to his purpose. But if he intend (as he doth) that there are no Lawes *de facto*, which are the ordinances of reason erring, instituted for the common hurt, and prescribing that which ought not to be done, he is much mistaken. *Pharaohs* Law to drown the Male Children of the *Israelites*, Exod. 1. 22. *Nebuchadnezzars* Law, that whosoever did not fall down and worship the golden image which he had set up, should be cast into the fiery furnace, *Dan.* 3. 4. *Darius* his Law, that whosoever should ask a Petition of any God or man, for thirty dayes, save of the King, should be cast into the Den of Lions, *Dan.* 6. 7. *Ahashuerosh* his Law, to destroy the Jewish Nation, root & branch, *Esther* 3. 13. The Pharisees Law, that whosoever confessed Christ, should be excommunicated, *John* 9. 22. were all unjust Lawes.

The ground of this errour is as great an errour it self (Such an art he hath learned of repacking Paradoxes) which is this. That *every man makes by his consent the Law which he is bound to keep*; If this were true, it would preserv them, if not from being unjust, yet from being injurious: But it is not true. The positive Law of God, conteined in the old and new Testament; The Law of Nature, written in our hearts by the Finger of God; The Lawes of Conquerors, who come in by the power of the Sword. The Lawes of our Ancestors, which were made before we were born, do all oblige us to the observation of them, yet to none of all these did we give our actuall consent. Over and above all these exceptions, he builds upon a wrong foundation, that all Magistrates at first, were elective; The first Governors were Fathers of Families; And when those petty Princes could not afford competent protection and security to their subjects, many of them did resign their severall and respective interests into the hands of one joint Father of the Country.

And though his ground had been true, that all first Legislators were elective, which is false, yet his superstructure fails, for it was done in hope and trust, that they would make just Laws. If Magistrates abuse this trust, and deceive the hopes of the people, by making Tyrranicall Lawes, yet it is without their consent. A precedent trust doth not justifie the subsequent errours and abuses of a Trustee. He who is duely elected a Legislator, may exercise his Legislative power unduely. The peoples implicite consent doth not render the Tyrannicall Lawes of their Legislators to be just.

But his chiefest answer is, that *an action forbidden*

bidden, though it proceed from necessary causes, yet if it were done willingly, it may be justly punished, which according to his custome he prooves by an instance ; *A man necessitated to steal by the strength of temptation, yet if he steal willingly, is justly put to death.* Here are two things, and both of them untrue.

First, he failes in his assertion. Indeed we suffer justly for those necessities which we our selves have contracted by our own fault, but not for extrinsecall, antecedent necesfities, which were imposed upon us without our fault. If that Law do not oblige to punishment which is not intimated, because the subject is invincibly ignorant of it ; How much less that Law which prescribes absolute impossibilities, unless perhaps invincible necessity be not as strong a plea as invincible ignorance. That which he addes, *if it were done willingly*, though it be of great moment, if it be rightly understood, yet in his sense, that is, if a mans *will be not in his own disposition*, and *if his willing do not come upon him according to his will, nor according to any thing els in his power*, it weighs not half so much as the least feather in all his horse-load. For if that Law be unjust and tyrannicall which commands a man to do that which is impossible for him to do, then that Law is likewise unjust and tyrannicall, which commands him to will that which is impossible for him to will.

Secondly, his instance supposeth an untruth, and is a plain begging of the question. No man is extrinsecally, antecedently and irresistibly necessitated cefsitated by temptation to steal. The Devill may follicite us, but he cannot necefsitate us. He hath a faculty of perswading, but not a power of compelling. *Nos ignem habemus, spiritus flammam ciet*, as *Nazianzen*. He blowes the coles, but the fire is our own. *Mordet duntaxat sese in fauces illius objicientem*, as St. *Austin*, he bites not untill we thrust our selves into his mouth. He may propose, he may suggest, but he cannot moove the will effectively. *Resist the Devill, and he will flie from you*, Jam. 4. 7. By faith we are able *to quench all the fiery darts of the wicked*, Eph. 6. 16. And if Sathan, who can both propose the object, and choose out the fittest times and places, to worke upon our frailties, and can suggest reasons, yet cannot necessitate the will (which is most certain,) then much less can outward objects do it alone. They have no naturall efficacy to determine the will. Well may they be occasions, but they cannot be causes of evill. The sensitive appetite may engender a proclivity to steal, but not a necessity to steal. And if it should produce a kind of necessity, yet it is but Moral, not Natural; Hypothetical, not Absolute; Coexistent, not Antecedent from our selves, nor Extrinsecall. This necessity, or rather proclivity, was free in its causes, we our selves by our own negligence in not opposing our passions when we should, and might, have freely given it a kind of dominion over us. Admit that some sudden passions may and do extraordinarily surprise us; And therefore we say, *motus primo primi*, the first motions are not always in

our

our power, neither are they free, yet this is but very rarely, and it is our own fault that they do surprise us. Neither doth the Law punish the first motion to theft, but the advised act of stealing. The intention makes the thief. But of this more largely numb. 25.

He pleades moreover, *that the Law is a cause of justice*, that it *frames the wills of men to justice*, and *that the punishment of one doth conduce to the preservation of many*. All this is most true, of a just Law justly executed. But this is no god-a-mercy to *T. H.* his opinion of absolute necessity. If all actions, and all events be predetermined Naturaly, Necessarily, Extrinsecally, how should the Law frame men morally to good actions? He leaves nothing for the Law to do, but either that which is done already, or that which is impossible to be done. If a man be chained to every individual act which he doth, and from every act which he doth not, by indissolvible bonds of inevitable necessity, how should the Law either deterre him or frame him? If a dog be chained fast to a post, the sight of a rod cannot draw him from it. Make a thousand Lawes, that the fire shall not burn, yet it will burn. And whatsoever men do (according to *T. H.*) they do it as necessarily, as the fire burneth. Hang up a thousand Theeves, and if a man be determined inevitably to steal, he must steal notwithstanding.

He addes, that *the sufferings imposed by the Law upon delinquents, respect not the evill act past, but the good to come*, and that *the putting of a delinquent to death by the Magistrate for any crime whatsoever*, cannot be justified before God, except there be a real intention to benefit others by his example. The truth is, the punishing of delinquents by Law, respecteth both the evill act past, and the good to come. The ground of it, is the evill act past, the scope or end of it, is the good to come. The end without the ground cannot justifie the act. A bad intention may make a good action bad; but a good intention cannot make a bad action good. It is not lawfull to do evill, that good may come of it, nor to punish an innocent person for the admonition of others; that is to fall into a certain crime, for fear of an uncertain. Again, though there were no other end of penalties inflicted, neither probatory, nor castigatory, nor exemplary, but only vindicatory, to satisfie the Law, out of a zeal of Justice, by giving to every one his own, yet the action is just and warrantable. Killing, as it is considered in it self without all undue circumstances, was never prohibited to the lawfull Magistrate, who is the Vicegerent or Lieutenant of God, from whom he derives his power of life and death.

T. H. hath one plea more. As a drowning man catcheth at every Bulrush, so he layes hold on every pretence to save a desperate cause. But first, it is worth our observation to see how oft he changeth shapes in this one particular. First, he told us, that it was the irresistible power of God that justifies all his actions, though he command one thing openly, and plot another thing
secretly,

secretly, though he be the cause, not only of the action, but also of the irregularity, though he both give man power to act and determine this power to evill, as well as good; though he punish the Creatures, for doing that which he himself did necessitate them to do. But being pressed with reason, that this is tyrannical; first, to necessitate a man to do his will, and then to punish him for doing of it, he leaves this pretence in the plain field, and flies to a second. That therefore a man is justly punished, for that which he was necessitated to do, because the act was voluntary on his part. This hath more shew of reason than the former, if he did make the will of man to be in his own disposition, but maintaining, that the will is irresistibly determined to will whatsoever it doth will, the injustice and absurdity is the same; First, to necessitate a man to will, and then to punish him for willing. The dog onely bites the stone which is thrown at him with a strange hand, but they make the first cause to punish the instrument, for that which is his own proper act. Wherefore not being satisfied with this, he casts it off, and flies to his third shift. *Men are not punished* (saith he) *therefore, because their theft proceeded from election* (that is, because it was willingly done, for to Elect and Will, saith he, are both one; Is not this to blow hot and cold with the same breath?) *but because it was noxious and contrary to mens preservation.* Thus far he saith true, that every creature by the instinct of nature, seeks to preserve it self; cast

water

water into a dusty place, and it contracts it self into little globes, that is, to preserve it self. And those who are noxious in the eye of the Law, are justly punished by them to whom the execution of the Law is committed; but the Law accounts no persons noxious, but those who are noxious by their own fault. It punisheth not a thorn for pricking, because it is the nature of the thorn, and it can do no otherwise, nor a child before it have the use of reason. If one should take mine hand perforce, and give another a box on the ear with it, my hand is noxious, but the Law punisheth the other who is faulty. And therefore he hath reason to propose the question, *how it is just to kill one man to amend another, if he who killed did nothing but what he was neeessitated to do.* He might as well demand how it is lawfull to murther a company of innocent Infants to make a bath of their lukewarm blood, for curing the Leprosy. It had been a more rational way; first, to have demonstrated that it is so, and then to have questioned why it is so. His assertion it self is but a dream, and the reason which he gives of it why it is so, is a dream of a dream.

The sum of it is this; *That where there is no Law, there no killing or any thing els can be unjust; that before the constitution of Commonwealths every man had power to kill another, if he conceived him to be hurtfull to him; that at the constitution of Commonwealths particular men lay down this right in part, and in part reserve it to themselves, as in case of theft, or murther.*

ther. That the right which the Commonwealth hath to put a malefactor to death is not created by the Law, but remaineth from the first right of Nature, which every man hath to preserve himself, that the killing of men in this case is as the killing of beasts in order to our own preservavation. This may well be called stringing of Paradoxes.

But first, there never was any such time when mankind was without Governors and Lawes, and Societies. Paternall Government was in the world from the beginning, and the Law of Nature. There might be sometimes a root of such Barbarous Theevish Brigants, in some rocks, or desarts, or odd corners of the world, but it was an abuse and a degeneration from the nature of man, who is a politicall creature. This savage opinion reflects too much upon the honour of mankind.

Secondly, there never was a time when it was lawfull ordinarily for private men to kill one another for their own preservation. If God would have had men live like wild beasts, as Lions, Bears or Tygers, he would have armed them with hornes, or tusks, or talons, or pricks; but of all creatures man is born most naked, without any weapon to defend himself, because God had provided a better means of security for him, that is, the Magistrate.

Thirdly, that right which private men have to preserve themselves, though it be with the killing of another, when they are set upon to be murdered or robbed, is not a remainder or a reserve

reserve of some greater power which they have resigned, but a privilege which God hath given them, in case of extreme danger and invincible necessity, that when they cannot possibly have recourse to the ordinary remedy, that is, the Magistrate, every man becomes a Magistrate to himself.

4. Fourthly, nothing can give that which it never had; The people, whilest they were a dispersed rabble (which in some odd cases might happen to be) never had justly the power of life and death, and therefore they could not give it by their election. All that they do is to prepare the matter, but it is God Almighty, that infuseth the soul of power.

5. Fiftly and lastly, I am sorry to hear a man of reason and parts to compare the murthering of men with the slaughtering of brute beasts. The elements are for the Plants, the Plants for the brute beasts, the brute beasts for man. When God inlarged his former grant to man, and gave him liberty to eat the flesh of the creatures for his sustenance, *Gen.* 9. 3. Yet man is expresly excepted, ver. 6. *Who so sheddeth mans blood, by man shall his blood be shed.* And the reason is assigned, *for in the Image of God made he man.* Before sin entred into the world, or before any creatures were hurtfull, or noxious to man, he had dominion over them, as their Lord and Master. And though the possession of this soveraignty be lost in part, for the sin of man, which made not onely the creatures to rebell, but also the inferiour faculties, to rebell against the superiour,

periour, from whence it comes, that one man is hurtfull to another, yet the dominion still remaines; wherein we may observe how sweetly the providence of God doth temper this cross, that though the strongest creatures have withdrawn their obedience, as Lions and Beares, to shew that man hath lost the excellency of his dominion, and the weakest creatures, as Flies and Gnats, to shew into what a degree of contempt he is fallen, yet still the most profitable and usefull creatures, as Sheep and Oxen, do in some degree retain their obedience.

The next branch of his answer concernes consultations, *which (saith he) are not superfluous, though all things come to pass necessarily, because they are the cause which doth necessitate the effect, and the means to bring it to pass.* We were told *Numb.* 11. that the last dictate of right reason was but as the last feather which breaks the horses back. It is well, yet that reason hath gained some command again, and is become at least a Quarter-master. Certainly if any thing under God have power to determin the will, it is right reason. But I have shewed sufficiently, that reason doth not determine the will Physically, nor absolutely, much less extrinsecally, and antecedently, and therefore it makes nothing for that necessity which *T. H.* hath undertaken to prove. He adds further, that *as the end is necessary, so are the means; And when it is determined, that one thing shall be chosen before another, it is determined also for what cause it shall be so chosen.* All which is

truth,

truth, but not the whole truth; for as God ordaines means for all ends, so he adapts and fits the means to their respective ends, free means to free ends, contingent means to contingent ends, necessary means to necessary ends, whereas T. H. would have all means, all ends, to be necessary. If good hath so ordered the world, that a man ought to use and may freely use those means of God, which he doth neglect, not by vertue of Gods decree, but by his own fault; If a man use those means of evill, which he ought not to use, and which by Gods decree, he had power to forbear; If God have left to man in part the free managery of human affaires, and to that purpose hath endowed him with understanding. then consultations are of use, then provident care is needfull, then it concerns him to use the means. But if God have so ordered this world, that a man cannot, if he would, neglect any means of good, which by vertue of Gods decree it is possible for him to use, and that he cannot possibly use any means of evill, but those which are irresistibly and inevitably imposed upon him by an antecedent decree, then not only consultations are vain, but that noble faculty of reason it self is vain: do we think that we can help God Almighty to do his proper work? In vain we trouble our selves, in vain we take care to use those means, which are not in our power to use, or not to use. And this is that which was conteined in my Prolepsis or prevention of his answer, though he be pleased both to disorder it, and to silence it. We cannot

not hope by our labours, to alter the courſe of things ſet down by God; let him perform his decree, let the neceſſary cauſes do their work. If we be thoſe cauſes, yet we are not in our own diſpoſition, we muſt do what we are ordained to do, and more we cannot do. Man hath no remedy but patience, and ſhrug up the ſhoulders. This is the doctrine flowes from this opinion of abſolute neceſſity. Let us ſuppoſe the great wheel of the clock which ſetts all the little wheels a going, to be as the decree of God, and that the motion of it were perpetual infallible from an intrinſecal principle, even as Gods decree is Infallible, Eternal, All-ſufficient. Let us ſuppoſe the leſſer wheels to be the ſecond cauſes, and that they do as certainly follow the motion of the great wheel, without miſſing or ſwerving in the leaſt degree, as the ſecond cauſes do purſue the determination of the firſt cauſe. I deſire to know in this caſe what cauſe there is to call a Councell of Smiths, to conſult and order the motion of that which was ordered and determined before their hands. Are men wiſer than God? yet all men know, that the motion of the leſſer wheels is a neceſſary means to make the clock ſtrike.

But he tells me in great ſadneſs, that *my argument is juſt like this other; If I ſhall live till to morrow, I ſhall live till to morrow, though I run my ſelf through with a ſword to day, which ſaith he, is a falſe conſequence, and a falſe propoſition*. Truly, if by running through, he underſtands killing, it is a falſe, or rather a fooliſh
propooſition

proposition, and implyes a contradiction. To live till to morrow, and to day to dy, are inconsistent. But by his favour, this is not my consequence, but this is his own opinion. He would perswade us, that it is absolutely necessary, that a man shall live till to morrow, and yet that it is possible that he may kill himself to day. My Argument is this. If there be a liberty and possibility for a man to kill himself to day, then it is not absolutely necessary, that he shall live till to morrow; but there is such a liberty, therefore no such necessity. And the consequence which I make here is this. If it be absolutely necessary, that a man shall live till to morrow, then it is vain and superfluous for him to consult and deliberate, whether he should dy to day, or not. And this is a true consequence; The ground of his mistake is this, that though it be true, that a man may kill himself to day, yet upon the supposition of his absolute necessity it is impossible. Such Heterogeneous arguments and instances he produceth, which are half builded upon our true grounds, and the other half upon his false grounds.

The next branch of my argument concerns Admonitions, to which he gives no new answer, and therefore I need not make any new reply; saving only to tell him, that he mistakes my argument; I say not only, If all things be necessary, then admonitions are in vain, but if all things be necessary, then it is to no more purpose to admonish men of understanding than fools, children, or mad-men. That they do admonish the
one

one and not the other, is confessedly true; and no reason under heaven can be given for it but this, that the former have the use of reason, and true liberty, with a dominion over their own actions, which children, fools and mad-men have not.

Concerning praise and dispraise, he inlargeth himself. The scope of his discourse is, that *things necessary may be praise-worthy*. There is no doubt of it, but withall their praise reflects upon the free agent, as the praise of a statue reflects upon the workman who made it. *To praise a thing* (saith he) *is to say, it is good*. True, but this goodness is not a Metaphysicall goodness, so the worst of things, and whatsoever hath a being, is good. Nor a natural goodness; The praise of it passeth wholy to the Author of Nature; God saw all that he had made, and it was very good. But a morall goodness, or a goodness of actions rather than of things. The morall goodness of an action is the conformity of it with right reason. The morall evill of an action, is the deformity of it, and the alienation of it from right reason. It is morall praise and dispraise which we speak of here. To praise any thing morally, is to say, it is morally good, that is, conformable to right reason. The morall dispraise of a thing is to say, it is morally bad, or disagreeing from the rule of right reason. So morall praise is from the good use of liberty, morall dispraise from the bad use of liberty: but if all things be necessary, than morall liberty is quite taken away, and with it all true praise and dispraise. Whereas *T. H.* adds, that *to say a thing* is good, is to say, it is *as I would wish, or as another would wish, or as the State would have it, or according to the Law of the Land*, he mistakes infinitely. He and another, and the State, may all wish, that which is not really good, but only in appearance. We do often wish what is profitable, or delightfull, without regarding so much as we ought what is honest. And though the will of the State where we live, or the Law of the Land do deserve great consideration, yet it is no infallible rule of morall goodnefs. And therefore to his question, *whether nothing that proceeds from necessity can please me*, I answer, yes. The burning of the fire pleaseth me when I am cold; And I say, it is good fire, or a creature created by God, for my use, and for my good: Yet I do not mean to attribute any morall goodnefs to the fire, nor give any morall praise to it, as if it were in the power of the fire it self, either to communicate its heat, or to suspend it, but I praise first the Creator of the fire, and then him who provided it. As for the praise which *Velleius Paterculus* gives *Cato*, that he was good by nature, *Et quia aliter esse non potuit*, it hath more of the Oratour than either of the Theologian or Philosopher in it. Man in the State of innocency did fall and become evill, what privilege hath *Cato* more than he? No, by his leave. *Narratur & dij Catonis sæpe mero caluisse virtus.* but the true meaning is, that he was naturally of a good temper, not so prone to some kinds of vices as others were; This is to praise a thing, not an action, naturally, not morally. *Socrates* was

not

not of so good a naturall temper, yet prooved as good a man; the more his praise, by how much the difficulty was the more to conform his disorderly appetite to right reason.

Concerning reward and punishment, he saith not a word, but onely that they frame and confound the will to good, which hath been sufficiently answered. They do so indeed, but if his opinion were true, they could not do so. But because my aim is not only to answer *T. H.* but also to satisfie my self; Though it be not urged by him, yet I do acknowledge, that I find some improper and analogicall rewards and punishments used to brute beasts, as the hunter rewards his dog, the master of the Coy-duck whipps her, when she returns without company. And if it be true, which he affirmeth a little before, that I have confessed, that *the actions of brute beasts are all necessitated and determined to that one thing which they shall do*, the difficulty is increased.

But first, my saying is misalleged. I said, that some kinds of actions which are most excellent in brute beasts, and make the greatest shew of reason, as the Bees working their Honey, and the Spiders weaving their Webbs, are yet done without any consultation, or deliberation, by a meer instinct of nature, and by a determination of their fancies, to these only kinds of workes But I did never say, I could not say, that all their individuall actions are necessary, and antecedently determined in their causes, as what dayes the Bees shall flie abroad, and what dayes and houres each Bee shall keep in the

Hive

Hive, how often they shall fetch in Thyme on a day, and from whence. These actions and the like, though they be not free, because brute beasts want reason to deliberate, yet they are contingent, and therefore not necessary.

2. Secondly, I do acknowledge, that as the fancies of some brute creatures are determined by nature, to some rare & exquisite works; So in others, where it finds a naturall propension; Art which is the Imitator of Nature, may frame & form them according to the will of the Artist, to some particular actions and ends, as we see in Setting-doggs, and Coy-ducks, and Parrots; and the principall means whereby they effect this, is by their backs, or by their bellies, by the rod, or by the morsell, which have indeed a shadow, or resemblance of rewards and punishments. But we take the word here properly, not as it is used by vulgar people, but as it is used by Divines and Philosophers, for that recompense which is due to honest and dishonest actions. Where there is no morall liberty, there is neither honesty nor dishonesty, neither true reward nor punishment.

3. Thirdly, when brute creatures do learn any such qualities, it is not out of judgment, or deliberation, or discourse, by inferring or concluding one thing from another, which they are not capable of. Neither are they able to conceive a reason of what they do, but meerly out of memory, or out of a sensitive fear, or hope. They remember, that when they did after one manner, they were beaten; and when they did after another manner, they were cherished, and accordingly

dingly they apply themselves. But if their individuall actions were absolutely necessary, fear or hope could not alter them. Most certainly, if there be any desert in it, or any praises due unto it, it is to them who did instruct them.

Lastly, concerning Arts, Arms, Books, Instruments, Study, Physick, and the like, he answereth not a word more than what is already satisfied. And therefore I am silent.

J. D.

THirdly, let this opinion be once radicated in the minds of men, that there is no true liberty, and that all things come to pass inevitably, and it will utterly destroy the Study of piety. Who will bewaile his sinns with teares? what will become of that Grief, that Zeal, that Indignation, that holy Revenge, which the Apostle speaks of, if men be once throughly persuaded that they could not shun what they did? A man may grieve for that which he could not help, but he will never be brought to bewail, that as his own fault, which flowed not from his own errour, but from an antecedent necessity. Who will be carefull or sollicitous to perform obedience, that believeth, there are inevitable bounds and limits set to all his devotions, which he can neither go beyond, nor come short of? To what end shall he pray God to avert those evills which are inevitable? or to confer those favours which are impossible? We indeed know not what good or evill shall happen to us, but this we know, that if all things be necessary, our devotions and indeavours cannot alter that which must be.

Numb. 15.
Arg. 3.

In a word, the onely reason why those persons who tread in this path of fatall destiny do sometimes pray, or repent, or serve God, is because the light of nature and the strength of reason, and the evidence of Scripture, do for that present transport them from their ill chosen grounds, and expell those Stoicall fancies out of their heads; A complete Stoick can neither pray, nor repent, nor serve God to any purpose. Either allow liberty, or destroy Church, as well as Commonwealth, Religion as well as Policy.

T. H.

His third Argument consisteth in other inconveniences which he saith will follow, namely, impiety & negligence of Religious duties, repentance and zeal to Gods service. To which I answer, as to the rest, that they follow not. I must confess, if we consider far the greatest part of mankind, not as they should be, but as they are, that is, as men whom either the study of acquiring wealth, or preferments, or whom the appetite of sensuall delights, or the impatience of meditating, or the rash imbracing of wrong principles, have made unapt to discuss the truth of things, that the dispute of this question will rather hurt than help their piety. And therefore, if he had not desired this answer, I would not have written it. Nor do I write it, but in hope your Lordship, and he will keep it in private. Nevertheless in very truth, the necessity of events does not of it self draw with it any impiety at all. For piety consisteth onely in two things; One, that we honour God in our hearts, which is, that we think of his power

power as highly as we can, for to honour any thing is nothing els but to think it to be of great power. The other, that we signifie that honour and esteem by our words and actions, which is called cultus, or worship of God. He therefore that thinketh that all things proceed from Gods Eternall Will, and consequently are necessary, does he not think God Omnipotent? does he not esteem of his power as highly as possible? which is to honour God as much as can be in his heart. Again, he that thinketh so, is he not more apt by externall acts and words to acknowledge it, then he that thinketh otherwise? Yet is this externall acknowledgement the same thing which we call worship. So this opinion fortifieth piety in both kinds, externally, internally, and therefore is far from destroying it. And for repentance, which is nothing but a glad returning into the right way, after the grief of being out of the way, though the cause that made him go astray were necessary, yet there is no reason why he should not grieve; and again, though the cause why he returned into the way were necessary, there remaines still the causes of joy. So that the necessity of the actions taketh away neither of those parts of repentance, grief for the errour, nor joy for the returning. And for prayer, whereas he saith, that the necessity of things destroyes prayer, I deny it. For though prayer be none of the causes that moove Gods will, his will being unchangeable, yet since we find in Gods Word, he will not give his blessings but to those that ask them, the motive to prayer is the same. Prayer is the gift of God, no

less

less than the blessings. And the prayer is decreed together in the same decree wherein the blessing is decreed. Tis manifest, that thanksgiving is no cause of the blessing past; And that which is past is sure, and necessary. Yet even amongst men, thanks is in use as an acknowledgment of the benefit past, though we should expect no new benefit for our gratitude. And prayer to God Almighty is but thanksgiving for his blessings in generall; and though it precede the particular thing we ask, yet it is not a cause or means of it, but a signification that we expect nothing but from God, in such manner as he, not as we will. And our Saviour by word of mouth bids us pray, Thy will, not our will be done, and by example teaches us the same, for he prayed thus, Father, if it be thy will, let this cup pass, &c. *The end of prayer, as of thanksgiving, is not to move, but to honour God Almighty, in acknowledging that what we ask can be effected by him only.*

J. D.

I Hope *T. H.* will be perswaded in time, that it is not the Covetousnefs, or Ambition, or Sensuallity, or Sloth, or Prejudice of his Readers which renders this doctrine of absolute necessity dangerous, but that it is in its own nature destructive to true godliness; And though his answer consist more of oppositions than of solutions, yet I will not willingly leave one grain of his matter unweighed. First, he erres in making inward piety to consist meerly in the estimation of the judgment. If this were so, what hinders but that the Devills should have

as

as much inward piety as the best Christians, for they esteem Gods power to be infinite, and tremble? Though inward piety do suppose the act of the understanding, yet it consisteth properly in the act of the will, being that branch of Justice which gives to God the honor which is due unto him. Is there no Love due to God, no Faith, no Hope? Secondly, he erres in making inward piety to ascribe no glory to God, but only the glory of his Power or Omnipotence. What shall become of all other the divine attributes, and particularly of his Goodness, of his Truth, of his Justice, of his mercy, which beget a more true and sincere honour in the heart than greatness it self? *Magnos facile laudamus, bonos lubenter.* Thirdly, this opinion of absolute necessity destroyes the truth of God, making him to command one thing openly, and to necessitate another privately, to chide a man for doing that which it hath determined him to do, to profess one thing, and to intend another. It destroyes the goodness of God, making him to be an hater of mankind, and to delight in the torments of his creatures, whereas the very doggs licked the sores of *Lazarus* in pitty and commiseration of him. It destroyes the Justice of God, making him to punish the creatures for that which was his own act, which they had no more power to shun, than the fire hath power not to burn. It destroyes the very power of God, making him to be the true Author of all the defects and evills which are in the world. These are the fruits of Impotence, not of Omnipotence. He who is

the

the effective cause of sin either in himselfe, or in the Creature, is not Almighty. There needs no other Devill in the world to raise jealousies and suspitions between God and his creatures, or to poison mankind with an apprehension, that God doth not love them, but onely this opinion, which was the office of the Serpent *Gen.* 3. 5. Fourthly, for the outward worship of God. How shall a man praise God for his goodness, who believes him to be a greater Tyrant than ever was in the world? who creates millions to burn eternally without their fault, to express his power? How shall a man hear the Word of God with that reverence, and devotion, and faith, which is requisite, who believeth that God causeth his Gospel to be preached to the much greater part of Christians, not with any intention that they should be converted and saved, but meerly to harden their hearts, and to make them inexcusable? How shall a man receive the blessed Sacrament with comfort and confidence, as a Seal of Gods love in Christ, who believeth, that so many millions are positively excluded from all fruit and benefit of the Passions of Christ, before they had done either good or evill? How shall he prepare himself with care and conscience, who apprehendeth, that Eating and Drinking unworthily is not the cause of damnation, but because God would damn a man, therefore he necessitates him to eat and drink unworthily? How shall a man make a free vow to God, without gross ridiculous hypocrisy, who thinks he is able to perform nothing, but as he

is

is extrinsecally necessitated? Fiftly, for Repentance, how shall a man condemn and accuse himself for his sins, who thinks himself to be like a Watch which is wound up by God, and that he can go neither longer nor shorter, faster nor slower, truer nor falser, than he is ordered by God? If God sets him right, he goes right. If God set him wrong, he goes wrong. How can a man be said to return into the right way, who never was in any other way, but that which God himself had chalked out for him? What is his purpose to amend, who is destitute of all power, but as if a man should purpose to fly without wings, or a begger who hath not a groat in his purse, purpose to build Hospitalls?

We use to say, admit one absurdity, and a thousand will follow. To maintain this unreasonable opinion of absolute necessity he is necessitated (but it is hypothetically, he might change his opinion, if he would) to deal with all antient Writers, as the *Goths* did with the *Romans*, who destroyed all their magnificent works, that there might remain no monument of their greatness upon the face of the earth. Therefore he will not leave so much as one of their opinions, nor one of their definitions, nay, not one of their tearmes of Art standing. Observe what a description he hath given us here of Repentance. *It is a glad returning into the right way, after the grief of being out of the way.* It amazed me to find *gladness* to be the first word in the description of repentance. His repentance is not that repentance, nor his piety that

that piety, nor his prayer that kind of prayer which the Church of God in all Ages hath acknowledged. Fasting, and Sackcloth, and Ashes, and Teares, and *Humi-cubations*, used to be companions of Repentance. Joy may be a consequent of it, not a part of it. It is a *returning*, but whose act is this returning? Is it Gods alone, or doth the penitent person concur also freely with the grace of God? If it be Gods alone, then it is his repentance, not mans repentance, what need the penitent person trouble himself about it? God will take care of his own work. The Scriptures teach us otherwise, that God expects our concurrence, Revel. 3. 19. *Be zealous and repent, behold I stand at the dore, and knock. If any man hear my voyce, and open the dore, I will come in to him.* It is a *glad returning into the right way.* Why dare any more call that a wrong way, which God himself hath determined? He that willeth, and doth that which God would have him to will and to do, is never out of his right way. It followes in his description, *after the grief, &c.* It is true, a man may grieve for that which is necessarily imposed upon him, but he cannot grieve for it as a fault of his own, if it never was in his power to shun it; Suppose a Writing-master shall hold his Scholars hand in his, and write with it; the Scholars part is only to hold still his hand, whether the Master write well or ill; the Scholar hath no ground, either of joy or sorrow as for himself, no man will interpret it to be his act, but his Masters. It is no fault to be out of the right

right way, if a man had not liberty to have kept himself in the way.

And so from *Repentance* he skipps quite over *New obedience*, to come to Prayer, which is the last Religious duty insisted upon by me here. But according to his use, without either answering or mentioning what I say. Which would have shewed him plainely what kind of prayer I intend, not contemplative prayer in generall, as it includes thanksgiving, but that most proper kind of prayer which we call *Petition*, which used to be thus defined, to be an *act of Religion by which we desire of God something which we have not, and hope that we shall obtain it by him*. Quite contrary to this *T. H.* tells us, that prayer *is not a cause, nor a meanes of Gods blessing, but only a signification that we expect it from him*. If he had told us onely that prayer is not a meritorious cause of Gods blessings, as the poor man by begging an almes doth not deserve it, I should have gone along with him. But to tell us, that it is not so much as a means to procure Gods blessing, and yet with the same breath, that *God will not give his blessings, but to those who pray*, who shall reconcile him to himself? The Scriptures teach us otherwise, *Whatsoever ye shall ask the Father in my Name, he will give it you*, John 16. 23. *Ask and it shall be given you, seek and ye shall find, knock and it shall be opened unto you*, Matth. 7.7. *St. Paul* tells the *Corinthians*, 2 Cor. 1.11. that he was *helped by their prayers*; thats not all, that *the gift was bestowed upon him by their means,*

means, So prayer is a *means*; And *St. James* saith, cap. 5. 16. *The effectuall fervent prayer of a righteous man availeth much.* If it be effectuall, then it is a cause. To shew this efficacy of prayer, our Saviour useth the comparison of a Father towards his Child, of a Neighbour towards his Neighbour, yea, of an unjust Judge, to shame those who think, that God hath not more compassion than a wicked man. This was signified by *Jacobs* wrestling and prevailing with God. Prayer is like the Tradesmans tools wherewithall he gets his living for himself, and his family. But, saith he, *Gods will is unchangeable.* What then? He might as well use this against study, Physick, and all second causes, as against Prayer. He shewes even in this, how little they attribute to the endeavours of men. There is a great difference between these two, *mutare voluntatem*, to change the will, which God never doth, in whom there is not the least shadow of turning by change; His will to love and hate, was the same from eternity, which it now is, and ever shall be. His love and hatred are immovable, but we are removed, *Non tellus cymbam tellurem cymba reliquit*, And *velle mutationem*, to will a change, which God often doth. To change the will argues a change in the Agent, but to will a change, only argues a change in the object. It is no inconstancy in a man to love or to hate, as the object is changed. *Præsta mihi omnia eadem & idem sum.* Prayer works not upon God, but us; It renders not him more propitious in himself, but us more capable

of

of mercy. He saith, this, *That God doth not bless us, except we pray, is a motive to prayer.* Why talks he of motives, who acknowledgeth no liberty, nor admitts any cause, but absolutely necessary? He saith, *Prayer is the gift of God, no less than the blessing which we pray for, and conteined in the same decree with the blessing.* It is true, the spirit of prayer is the gift of God, will he conclude from thence, that the good imployment of one talent, or of one gift of God, may not procure another? Our Saviour teacheth us otherwise, *Come thou good and faithfull servant, thou hast been faithfull in little, I will make thee ruler over much.* Too much light is an enemy to the light, and too much Law is an enemy to Justice. I could wish we wrangled less about Gods Decrees, untill we understood them better. But, saith he, Thanksgiving is no cause of the blessing past, and prayer is but a thanksgiving. He might even as well tell me, that when a beggar craves an almes, and when he gives thanks for it, it is all one. Every thanksgiving is a kind of prayer, but every prayer, and namely Petition, is not a thanks-giving. In the last place he urgeth, that *in our prayers we are bound, to submit our wills to Gods Will*, who ever made any doubt of this, we must submit to the Preceptive will of God, or his Commandments; we must submit to the effective Will of God, when he declares his good pleasure by the event or otherwise. But we deny, and deny again, either that God wills things, *ad extra*, without himself necessarily, or that it is his pleasure that all second causes should act necessarily at all times, which is the question, and that which he allegeth to the contrary comes not neer it.

J. D.

Numb. 16.
Arg. 4.

Fourthly, the order, beauty and perfection of the world doth require, that in the Universe should be Agents of all sorts, some necessary, some free, some contingent. He that shall make either all things necessary, guided by destiny; or all things free, governed by election; or all things contingent, happening by chance, doth overthrow the beauty and the perfection of the world.

T. H.

THE fourth Argument from reason is this, The Order, Beauty and Perfection of the world requireth, that in the Universe, should be Agents of all sorts, some necessary, some free, some contingent. He that shall make all things necessary, or all things free, or all things contingent, doth overthrow the beauty and perfection of the world.

In which Argument I observe, first, a contradiction. For, seeing he that maketh any thing in that he maketh it, he maketh it to be necessary, it followeth, that he that maketh all things, maketh all things necessary to be. As if a workman make a garment, the garment must necessarily be. So if God make every thing, every thing must necessarily be. Perhaps the beauty of the world requireth (though we know it not) that some Agents should work without deliberation,
which

which he calls necessary Agents. And some Agents with deliberation, and those, both he and I, call free Agents. And that some Agents should work, and we not know how; And them effects we both call contingent; But this hinders not, but that he that electeth may have his election necessarily determined to one by former causes; And that which is contingent and imputed to Fortune, be nevertheless necessary, and depend on precedent necessary causes. For by contingent, men do not mean that which hath no cause, but which hath not for cause any thing which we perceive. As for example; when a Travailer meets with a shower, the journey had a cause, and the rain had a cause sufficient enough to produce it, but because the journey caused not the rain, nor the rain the journey, we say, they were contingent one to another. And thus you see, though there be three sorts of events, Necessary, Contingent, and Free, yet they may be all necessary, without the destruction of the beauty or perfection of the Univers.

J. D.

THE first thing he observes in mine Argument is contradiction, as he calls it, but in truth it is but a deception of the sight. As one candle sometimes seems to be two, or a rod in the water shewes to be two rods, *Quicquid recipitur, recipitur ad modum recipientis.* But what is this contradiction? Because I say, he who maketh all things, doth not make them necessary: What a contradiction, and but one proposition? That were strange. I say, God hath not made

K all

all Agents neceſſary, he faith, God hath made all Agents neceſſary. Here is a contradiction indeed, but it is between him and me, not between me and my ſelf. But yet though it be not a formall contradiction, yet perhaps it may imply a contradiction *in adjecto*. Wherefore to clear the matter, and diſpell the miſt which he hath raiſed; It is true, that every thing when it is made, it is neceſſary that it be made ſo as it is, that is, by a neceſſity of infallibility, or ſuppoſition, ſuppoſing, that it be ſo made, but this is not that abſolute, antecedent neceſſity, whereof the queſtion is between him and me. As to uſe his own inſtance; Before the Garment be made, the Tailor is free to make it, either of the *Italian*, *Spaniſh*, or *French* faſhion indifferently: But after it is made, it is neceſſary that it be of that faſhion whereof he hath made it, that is by a neceſſity of ſuppoſition. But this doth neither hinder the cauſe from being a free cauſe, nor the effect from being a free effect, but the one did produce freely, and the other was freely produced. So the contradiction is vaniſhed.

In the ſecond part of his anſwer he grants, that there are ſome free Agents, and ſome contingent Agents, and that perhaps the beauty of the world doth require it, but like a ſhrewd Cow, which after ſhe hath given her milk, caſts it down with her foot, in the concluſion he tells us, that nevertheleſs they are all neceſſary. This part of his anſwer is a meer Logomachy, (as a great part of the controverſies in the world are) or a contention about words. What is the meaning

-ning of *necessary*, and free, and contingent actions. I have shewed before what free and necessary, do properly signifie, but he misrecites it. He faith, I make all Agents which want deliberation to be necessary, but I acknowledge that many of them are contingent. Neither do I approove his definition of contingents, though he say, I concur with him, that they are *such agents as work we know not how*. For according to this description many necessary actions should be contingent, and many contingent actions should be necessary. The Loadstone draweth Iron, the Jet chaff, we know not how, and yet the effect is necessary, and so it is in all Sympathies and Antipathies or occult qualities. Again, a man walking in the streets, a Tile falls down from an house, and breaks his head. We know all the causes, we know how this came to pass. The man walked that way, the pin failed, the Tile fell just when he was under it; And yet this is a contingent effect. The man might not have walked that way, and then the Tile had not fallen upon him. Neither yet do I understand here in this place by contingents, such events as happen besides the scope, or intention of the Agents; as when a man digging to make a grave, finds a Treasure, though the word be sometimes so taken. But by contingents, I understand all things which may be done, and may not be done, may happen or may not happen, by reason of the in determination, or accidentall concurrence of the causes. And those same things which are absolutely Incontingent and yet Hy-

K 2   pothetically

pothetically necessary. As supposing the Passenger did walk just that way, just at that time, and that the pin did fail just then, and the Tile fall, it was necessary that it should fall upon the Passengers head. The same defence will keep out his shower of rain. But we shall meet with his shower of rain again, Numb. 34. Whither I refer the further explication of this point.

J. D.

Numb. 17.
Arg. 5.

FIftly, take away liberty, and you take away the very nature of evill, and the formall reason of sin. If the hand of the Painter were the law of painting, or the hand of the Writer the law of writing, whatsoever the one did write, or the other paint, must infallibly be good. Seeing therefore, that the first cause is the rule and Law of goodness, if it do necessitate the will, or the person to evill, either by it self immediatly or mediatly, by necessary flux of second causes, it will no longer be evill. The essence of sin consists in this, that one commit that which he might avoid. If there be no liberty to produce sin, there is no such thing as sin in the world. Therefore it appeares, both from Scripture and reason, that there is true Liberty.

T. H.

TO the fift Argument from reason, which is, that if liberty be taken away, the nature and formall reason of sin is taken away, I answer, by denying the consequence. The nature of sin consisteth in this, that the action done proceed from our will, and be against the Law. A Judge in judging

judging whether it be sin or not, which is done against the Law, looks at no higher cause of the action then the will of the doer. Now when I say the action was necessary, I do not say it was done against the will of the doer, but with his will, and so necessarily, because mans will, that is, every act of the will, and purpose of man had a sufficient and therefore a necessary cause, and consequently every voluntary action was necessitated. An action therefore may be voluntary and a sin, and neverthelefs be necessary. And because God may afflict by right derived from his Omnipotency, though sin were not. And the example of punishment on voluntary sinners, is the cause that produceth Justice, and maketh sin less frequent. For God to punish such sinners, as I have shewed before, is no injustice. And thus you have my answer to his objections, both out of Scripture and reason.

J. D.

SCis tu simulare cupressum, quid hoc? It was shrewd counsail which *Alcibiades* gave to *Themistocles*, when he was busy about his accounts to the State, that he should rather study how to make no accounts. So it seemes *T. H.* thinks it a more compendious way to baulk an argument, then to satisfie it. And if he can produce a *Rowland* against an *Oliver*, if he can urge a reason against a reason, he thinks he hath quitted himself fairely. But it will not serve his turn. And that he may not complain of misunderstanding it, as those who have a politick deafness, to hear nothing but what liketh them, I will

will first reduce mine argument into form, and then weigh what he saith in answer, or rather in opposition to it. That opinion which takes away the formall reason of sin, and by consequence, sin it self, is not to be approoved; this is cleer, because both Reason and Religion, Nature, and Scripture do proove, and the whole world confesseth, that there is sin. But this opinion of the necessity of all things, by reason of a conflux of second causes, ordered and determined by the first cause, doth take away the very formall reason of sin; This is prooved thus. That which makes sin it self to be good, and just, and lawfull, takes away the formall cause, and distroyes the essence of sin; for if sin be good, and just, and lawfull, it is no more evill, it is no sin, no anomy. But this opinion of the necessity of all things, makes sin to be very good and just, and lawfull; for nothing can flow essentially by way of Physicall determination from the first cause, which is the Law and Rule of Goodness and Justice, but that which is good, and just, and lawfull, but this opinion makes sin to proceed essentially by way of Physicall determination from the first cause, as appeares in *T. H.* his whole discourse. Neither is it materiall at all, whether it proceed immediatly from the first cause, or mediately, so as it be by a necessary flux of second and determinate causes which produce it inevitably. To these proofs he answers nothing, but onely by denying the first consequence, as he calls it, and then sings over his old song, *That the nature of sin consi-*
steth

steth in this, that the action proceeds from our *will, and be against the Law*, which in our sense is most true, if he understand a just Law, and a free rationall will; But supposing (as he doth) that the Law injoines things impossible in themselves to be done, then it is an unjust and Tyrannicall Law, and the transgression of it is no sin, not to do that which never was in our power to do. And supposing likewise (as he doth) that the will is inevitably determined by speciall influence from the first cause, then it is not mans will, but Gods Will, and flowes essentually from the Law of Goodness.

That which he addes of a Judge, is altogether impertinent, as to his defence. Neither is a Civill Judge the proper Judge, nor the Law of the Land the proper Rule of Sin. But it makes strongly against him; for the Judge goes upon a good ground, and even this which he confesseth, that the *Judge looks at no higher cause, then the will of the doer*, prooves, that the will of the doer did determine it self freely, and that the malefactor had liberty to have kept the Law, if he would: Certainly, a Judge ought to look at all materiall circumstances, and much more at all essentiall causes. Whether every sufficient cause be a necessary cause, will come to be examined more properly, Numb. 31. For the present, it shall suffice to say, that liberty flowes from the sufficiency, and contingency from the debility of the cause. Nature never intends the generation of a monster. If all the causes concur sufficiently, a perfect creature is produced, but by reason of the

the insufficiency, or debility, or contingent aberration of some of the causes, sometimes a Monster is produced. Yet the causes of a Monster were sufficient for the production of that which was produced, that is a Monster, otherwise a Monster had not been produced. What is it then? A Monster is not produced by vertue of that order which is set in Nature, but by the contingent aberration of some of the naturall causes in their concurrence. The order set in Nature, is, that every like should beget its like. But supposing the concurrence of the causes to be such as it is, in the generation of a Monster, the generation of a Monster is necessary; as all the events in the world are when they are, that is, by an hypotheticall necessity. Then he betakes himself to his old help, that God may punish by right of omnipotence, though there were no sin. The question is not now what God may do, but what God will do, according to that Covenant which he hath made with man, *Fac hoc & vives*, Do this and thou shalt live, whether God doth punish any man contrary to this Covenant, *Hosea.* 13.9. *O Israel, thy destruction is from thy self, but in me is thy help*. He that wills not the death of a Sinner, doth much less will the death of an innocent Creature. By *death* or *destruction* in this discourse, the onely separation of Soul and Body is not intended, which is a debt of nature, and which God, as Lord of Life and Death, may justly do, and make it not a punishment, but a blessing to the party; but we understand the subjecting of the Creature to

eternall

eternall torments. Lastly, he tells of that benefit which redounds to others from Exemplary Justice, which is most true, but not according to his own grounds, for neither is it Justice to punish a man for doing that which it was impossible alwayes for him not to do; Neither is it lawfull to punish an innocent person, that good may come of it; And if his opinion of absolute necessity of all things were true, the destinies of men could not be altered, either by examples or fear of punishment.

J. D.

Numb. 18.

BUt the Patrons of necessity being driven out of the plain field with reason, have certain retreats or distinctions, which they fly unto for refuge. First, they distinguish between Stoicall necessity and Christian necessity, between which they make a threefold difference.

First, say they, the Stoicks did subject *Jupiter* to destiny, but we subject destiny to God; I answer, that the Stoicall and Christian destiny are one, and the same, *fatum quasi effatum Jovis*. Hear Seneca, *Destiny is the necessity of all things, and actions, depending upon the disposition of Jupiter*, &c. I add, that the Stoicks left a greater liberty to *Jupiter* over destiny, than these Stoicall Christians do to God over his decrees, either for the beginnings of things as *Euripides*, or for the progress of of them as *Chrysippus*, or at least of the circumstances of time and place, as all of them generally, So *Virgil*, *Sed trahere & moras ducere*, &c. So *Osyris* in *Apuleius*, promiseth him to prolong

prolong his life *Ultra fato constituta tempora*, beyond the times set down by the destinies.

2   Next, they say, that the Stoicks did hold an eternall flux and necessary connexion of causes, but they believe that God doth act, *prater & contra naturam*, besides and against nature. I answer, that it is not much materiall, whether they attribute necessity to God, or to the Starrs, or to a connexion of causes, so as they establish necessity. The former reasons do not onely condemn the ground or foundation of necessity, but much more necessity it self upon what ground soever. Either they must run into this absurdity, that the effect is determined, the cause remaining undetermined, or els hold such a necessary connexion of causes, as the Stoicks did.

3   Lastly, they say, the Stoicks did take away liberty and contingence, but they admit it; I answer, what liberty or contingence was it they admit, but a titular liberty, and an empty shadow of contingence? who do profess stifly, that all actions and events which either are or shall be, cannot but be, nor can be otherwise, after any other manner, in any other Place, Time, Number, Order, Measure, nor to any other end than they are, and that in respect of God, determining them to one; what a poor ridiculous liberty, or contingence is this?

Secondly, they distinguish between the first cause, and the second causes; they say, that in respect of the second causes many things are free,

free, but in respect of the first cause, all things are necessary. This answer may be taken away two wayes.

First, so contraries shall be true together; The same thing at the same time shall be determined to one, and not determined to one; the same thing at the same time must necessarily be, and yet may not be. Perhaps they will say, not in the same respect. But that which strikes at the root of this question is this, If all the causes were onely collaterall, this exception might have some colour, but where all the causes being joined together, and subordinate one to another, do make but one totall cause, if any one cause (much more the first) in the whole series, or subordination of causes be necessary, it determines the rest, and without doubt, makes the effect necessary; Necessity or Liberty is not to be esteemed from one cause, but from all the causes joyned together. If one link in a chain be fast, it fastens all the rest.

Secondly, I would have them tell me whether the second causes be predetermined by the first cause or not; If it be determined, then the effect is necessary, even in respect of the second causes; If the second cause be not determined, how is the effect determined, the second cause remaining undetermined? Nothing can give that to another which it hath not it self. But say they, nevertheless the power or faculty remaineth free. True, but not in order to the act, if it be once determined. It is free, *in sensu diviso*, but not *in sensu composito*, when a man

holds

holds a bird fast in his hand, is she therefore free to flie where she will, because she hath wings? Or a man imprisoned or fettered, is he therefore free to walk where he will, because he hath feet and a low motive faculty? Judge without prejudice, what a miserable subterfuge is this, which many men confide so much in.

T. H.

Certain distinctions which he supposing may be brought to his arguments are by him remooved.

HE saith, a man may perhaps answer, that the necessity of things held by him, is not a Stoicall necessity, but a Christian necessity, &c. but this distinction I have not used, nor indeed have ever heard before. Nor do I think any man could make Stoical and Christian two kinds of necessities, though they may be two kinds of doctrin. Nor have I drawn my answer to his arguments from the authority of any Sect, but from the nature of the things themselves.

But here I must take notice of certain words of his in this place, as making against his own Tenet, where all the causes, saith he, being joyned together, and subordinate one to another, do make but one totall cause; If any one cause, much more the first, in the whole series of subordination of causes be necessary, it determines the rest, and without doubt maketh the effect necessary. For, that which I call the necessary cause of any effect,

is

is the joyning together of all causes subordinate to the first into one totall cause. If any one of those, saith he, especially the first, produce its effect necessarily, then all the rest are determined, and the effect also necessary. Now, it is manifest, that the first cause is a necessary cause of all the effects that are next, and immediat to it, and therefore by his own reason, all effects are necessary. *Nor is that distinction of necessary, in respect of the first cause, and necessary in respect of second causes mine; It does* (as he well noteth) *imply a contradiction.*

J. D.

Because *T. H.* disavowes these two distinctions, I have joyned them together in one paragraph. He likes not the distinction of necessity or destiny, into Stoicall and Christian, no more do I. We agree in the conclusion, but our motives are diverse. My reason is, because I acknowledge no such necessity, either as the one or as the other, and because I conceive, that those Christian writers, who do justly detest the naked destiny of the Stoicks, as fearing to fall into those gross absurdities and pernicious consequences which flow from thence, do yet privily (though perhaps unwittingly) under another form of expression, introduce it again at the backdore after they had openly cast it out at the foredore: But *T. H.* rusheth boldly without distinctions (which he acccunts but Jargon) and without foresight upon the grossest destiny of all others, that is, that of the Stoicks. He confesseth, that *they may be two kinds of doctrine.*

May

May be? Nay, they are without all peradventure. And he himself is the first who beares the name of a Christian that I have read, that hath raised this sleeping Ghost out of its grave, and set it out in its true colours. But yet he likes not the names of Stoicall and Christian destiny, I do not blame him, though he would not willingly be accounted a Stoick. To admit the thing, and quarrell about the name, is to make our selves ridiculous. Why might not I first call that kind of destiny, which is maintained by Christians, Christian destiny? and that other maintained by Stoicks, Stoicall destiny? But I am not the inventer of the tearme. If he had been as carefull in reading other mens opinions, as he is confident in setting down his own, he might have found not only the thing, but the name it self often used. But if the name of *fatum Christianum*, do offend him, Let him call it with Lipsius, *fatum verum*, who divides destiny into four kinds; 1. Mathematicall or Astrologicall destiny, 2. Naturall destiny, 3. Stoicall or violent destiny; and 4. true destiny, which he calls ordinarily *nostrum*, our destiny; that is, of Christians, and *fatum pium*, that is godly destiny, and defines it just as *T. H.* doth his destiny, to be a series or order of causes depending upon the divine Counsail, *de conft. l.* 1. *cap.* 17. 18. & 19. Though he be more cautelous than *T. H.* to decline those rocks which some others have made shipwrack upon. Yet the Divines thought he came too neer them, as appeares by his Epistle to the Reader, in a later Edition. And by that

note

note in the margent of his twentieth Chapter, *whatsoever I dispute here, I submit to the judgment of the wise, and being admonished, I will convert it. One may convince me of error, but not of obstinacy.* So fearfull was he to overshoot himself, and yet he maintained both true liberty, and true contingency. *T. H.* saith, *he hath not sucked his answer from any Sect*; And I say so much the worse; It is better to be the disciple of an old Sect, than the ringleader of a new.

Concerning the other destinction of liberty, in respect of the first cause, and liberty in respect of the second causes, though he will not see that which it concerned him to answer, like those old *Damiæ*, which could put out their eyes when they list; As namely, that the faculty of willing, when it is determined in order to the act (which is all the freedom that he acknowledgeth) is but like the freedom of a bird, when she is first in a mans hand, &c. Yet he hath espied another thing wherein I contradict my self, because I affirm, that if any one cause in the whole series of causes, much more the first cause, be necessary, it determineth the rest. But, saith he, it is manifest, that the first cause is a necessary cause of all the effects that are next. I am glad, yet it is not I who contradict my self, but it is one of his *manifest truths* which I contradict. That *the first cause is a necessary cause of all effects*, which I say, is a manifest falshood. Those things which God wills without himself, he wills freely not necessarily. Whatsoever cause acts or works

necessarily

(144)

necessarily, doth act or work all that it can do, or all that is in its power; But it is evident, that God doth not all things without himself, which he can do, or which he hath power to do. He could have raised up children unto *Abraham* of the very stones, which were upon the banks of *Jordan, Luk.* 3. 8. but he did not. He could have sent twelve Legions of Angells to the succour of Christ, but he did not. *Matth.* 26. 53. God can make *T. H.* live the years of *Methuselah*, but it is not necessary that he shall do so, nor probable that he will do so. The productive power of God is infinite, but the whole created world is finite. And therefore God might still produce more, if it pleased him. But this it is, when men go on in a confused way, and will admit no distinctions. If *T. H.* had considered the difference between a necessary being, and a necessary cause, or between those actions of God, which are imminent within himself, and the transient works of God, which are extrinsecall without himself, he would never have proposed such an evident error, for a manifest truth. *Qui pauca considerat, facile pronuntiat.*

J. D.

Numb. 19. THirdly, they distinguish between liberty from compulsion, and liberty from necessitation. The Will, say they, is free from compulsion, but not free from necessitation. And this they fortifie with two reasons. First, because it is granted by all Divines, that hypotheticall necessity, or necessity upon a supposition, may consist with liberty; Secondly, because God and the

the good Angells do good neceſſarily, and yet are more free than we. To the firſt reaſon I confeſs, that neceſſity upon a ſuppoſition may ſometimes conſiſt with true liberty, as when it ſignifies onely an infallible certitude of the underſtanding in that which it knowes to be, or that it ſhall be; But if the ſuppoſition be not in the Agents power, nor depend upon any thing that is in his power; If there be an exteriour antecedent cauſe which doth neceſſitate the effect, to call this free, is to be mad with reaſon.

To the ſecond reaſon, I confeſs that God and the good Angells are more free than we are, that is, intenſively in the degree of freedom, but not extenſively in the latitude of the object, according to a liberty of exerciſe, but not of ſpecification. A liberty of exerciſe, that is, to doe or not to do, may conſiſt well with a neceſſity of ſpecification, or a determination to the doing of good. But a liberty of exerciſe, and a neceſſity of exerciſe; A liberty of ſpecification; and a neceſſity of ſpecification, are not compatible, nor can conſiſt together. He that is antecedently neceſſitated to do evill, is not free to do good. So this inſtance is nothing at all to the purpoſe.

T. H.

But the diſtinction of free, into free from compulſion, and free from neceſſitation, I acknowledge; for to be free from compulſion, is to do a thing ſo, as terrour be not the cauſe of his will to do it, for a man is then onely ſaid to be compelled, when fear makes him willing to it, as when a

man

man willingly throwes his goods into the Sea to save himself, or submitts to his enemy for fear of being killed. Thus all men that do any thing from love, or revenge, or lust are free from compulsion, and yet their actions may be as necessary as those which are done upon compulsion, for sometimes other passions work as forcibly as fear; But free from necessitation I say nothing can be; And 'tis that which he undertook to disproove. This distinction, he sayes, useth to be fortified by two reasons, but they are not mine. The first, he sayes is, That it is granted by all Divines, that an hypotheticall necessity, or necessity upon supposition, may stand with liberty. That you may understand this, I will give you an example of hypotheticall necessity. If I shall live, I shall eat, this is an hypotheticall necessity. Indeed it is a necessary proposition, that is to say, it is necessary that that proposition should be true, whensoever uttered, but tis not the necessity of the thing, nor is it therefore necessary, that the man shall live, or that the man shall eat. I do not use to fortifie my distinctions with such reasons. Let him confute them as he will, it contents me. But I would have your Lordship take notice hereby, how an easy and plain thing, but withall false, may be with the grave usage of such tearmes, as hypotheticall necessity, and necessity upon supposition and such like tearmes of Schoolemen, obscur'd and made to seem profound learning.

The second reason that may confirm the distinction of free from compulsion, and free from necessitation, he sayes is, that God, and good Angells
do

do good necessarily, and yet are more free than we. The reason, though I had no need of, yet I think it so far forth good, as it is true, that God and good Angells do good necessarily, and yet are free; but because I find not in the Articles of our faith, nor in the Decrees of our Church set down, in what manner I am to conceive God, and good Angells to work, by necessity, or in what sense they work freely, I suspend my sentence in that point, and am content, that there may be a freedom from compulsion, and yet no freedom from necessitation, as hath been prooved in that, that a man may be necessitated to some actions without threats and without fear of danger; But how he can avoid the consisting together of freedom and necessity, supposing God and good Angells are freer than men, and yet do good necessarily, that we must now examin.

I confess (saith he) that God and good Angells are more free than we, that is, intensively in degree of freedom, not extensively in the latitude of the object, according to a liberty of exercise, not of specification. Again, we have here two distinctions, that are no distinctions, but made to seem so by tearmes invented, by I know not whom, to cover ignorance, and blind the understanding of the Reader. For it cannot be conceived that there is any liberty greater than for a man to do what he will, and to forbear what he will. One heat may be more intensive than another, but not one liberty than another. He that can do what he will, hath all liberty possibly, and he that cannot, has none at all. Also liberty (as

he

he sayes, the Schooles call it) of exercise, which is as I have said before, a liberty to do, or not to do, cannot be without a liberty (which they call of specification) that is to say, a liberty to do or not to do, this or that in particular; for how can a man conceive, that he has liberty to do any thing, that hath not liberty to do this or that, or somewhat in particular. If a man be forbidden in Lent to eat this and that, and every other particular kind of flesh, how can he be understood to have a liberty to eat flesh, more than he that hath no license at all?

You may by this again see the vanity of distinctions used in the Schooles; And I do not doubt but that the imposing of them by authority of Doctours in the Church, hath been a great cause that men have laboured, though by sedition, and evill courses to shake them off; for nothing is more apt to beget hatred, than the tyrannising over mans reason and understanding, especially when it is done, not by the Scripture, but by pretense of learning, and more judgment than that of other men.

J. D.

HE who will speak with some of our great undertakers, about the grounds of learning, had need either to speak by an Interpreter, or to learn a new Language, (I dare not call it Jargon or Canting) lately devised, not to set forth the truth, but to conceal falshood. He must learn a new Liberty, a new Necessity, a new Contingency, a new Sufficiency, a new Spontaneity,

Spontaneity, a new kind of Deliberation, a new kind of Election, a new Eternity, a new Compulsion, and in conclusion, a new Nothing. This proposition, *the will is free*, may be understood in two senses, Either that the will is not compelled, or that the will is not alwayes necessitated, for if it be ordinarily, or at any time free from necessitation, my assertion is true, that there is freedom from necessity. The former sense, that the will is not compelled, is acknowledged by all the world as a truth undeniable; *Voluntas non cogitur*. For, if the will may be compelled, then it may both will and not will the same thing at the same time, under the same notion, but this implies a contradiction. Yet this Author (like the good woman whom her husband sought up the stream when she was drowned, upon pretense that when she was living, she used to go contrary courses to all other people,) he holds, that true compulsion and fear, may make a man will, that which he doth not will, that is, in his sense may compell the will. As when a man willingly throwes his goods into the Sea to save himself, or submits to his enemy for fear of being killed, I answer, that *T. H.* mistakes sundry wayes in this discourse.

First, he erreth in this, to think, that actions proceeding from fear, are properly compulsory actions, which in truth are not only voluntary, but free actions; neither compelled, nor so much as Physically necessitated. Another man, at the same time, in the same Ship, in the same storm, may choose, and the same individuall man otherwise

wise advised, might choose, not to throw his goods overboard. It is the man himself, who chooseth freely this means to preserve his life. It is true, that if he were not in such a condition, or if he were freed from the grounds of his present fears, he would not choose neither the casting of his goods into the Sea, nor the submitting to his enemy. But considering the present exigence of his affaires, reason dictates to him, that of two inconveniences, the less is to be chosen, as a comparative good. Neither doth he will this course, as the end or direct object of his desires, but as the means to attaine his end. And what Fear doth in these cases, Love, Hope, Hatred, &c. may do in other cases, that is, may occasion a man to elect those means to obtain his willed end, which otherwise he would not elect. As *Jacob* to serve seven years more, rather than not to enjoy his beloved *Rachel*. The Merchant to hazard himself upon the rough Seas, in hope of profit. Passions may be so violent, that they may necessitate the will, that is, when they prevent deliberations, but this is rarely, and then the will is not free. But they never properly compell it. That which is compelled, is against the will, and that which is against the will, is not willed.

2   Secondly, *T. H.* erres in this also, where he saith, that *a man is then onely said to be compelled when fear makes him willing to an action.* As if force were not more prevalent with a man then fear; we must know therefore, that this word *compelled* is taken two wayes, sometimes improperly,

perly, that is, when a man is mooved or occasioned by threats or fear, or any passion, to do that which he would not have done, if that threats, or that passion had not been; Sometimes it is taken properly, when we do any thing against our own inclination, mooved by an externall cause, the will not consenting, nor concurring, but resisting as much as it can. As in a Rape, or when a Christian is drawn or carried by violence to the Idolls Temple. Or as in the case of St. Peter, John 21.18. *Another shall guide thee, and carry thee whither thou wouldst not.* This is that compulsion which is understood, when we say, the will may be letted, or changed, or necessitated, or that the imperate actions of the will (that is, the actions of the inferiour faculties which are ordinarily moved by the will) may be compelled; but that the immanent actions of the will, that is, to will, to choose, cannot be compelled, because it is the nature of an action properly compelled to be done by an extrinsecall cause, without the concurrence of the will.

Thirdly, the question is not, whether all the actions of a man be free, but whether they be ordinarily free. Suppose some passions are so suddaine and violent, that they surprise a man, and betray the succours of the soul, and prevent deliberation, as we see in some *motus primo primi*; or antipathies, how some men will run upon the most dangerous objects, upon the first view of a loathed creature, without any power to contain themselves. Such actions as these, as

they

they are not ordinary, so they are not free, because there is no deliberation nor election. But where deliberation and election are, as when a man throwes his goods over-board, to save the Ship, or submitts to his enemy, to save his life; there is alwayes true liberty.

Though *T. H.* slight the two reasons which I produce in favour of his cause, yet they who urged them, deserved not to be slighted, unless it were because they were School-men. The former reason is thus framed; A necessity of supposition may consist with true liberty, but that necessity which flowes from the naturall and extrinsecall determination of the will, is a necessity of supposition; To this, my answer is in effect; That a necessity of supposition is of two kinds, sometimes the thing supposed is in the power of the Agent to do, or not to do; As for a Romish Priest to vow continence, upon supposition that he be a Romish Priest, is necessary, but because it was in his power to be a Priest, or not to be a Priest, therefore his vow is a free act. So supposing a man to have taken Physick, it is necessary that he keep at home, yet because it was in his power to take a Medicine or not to take it, therefore his keeping at home is free. Again, sometimes the thing supposed is not in the power of the Agent to do, or not to do; supposing a man to be extrem sick, it is necessary that he keep at home, or supposing that a man hath a naturall antipathy against a Cat, he runs necessarily away so soon as he sees her. Because this antipathy, and this sicknefs are not in the power

of

of the party affected, therefore these acts are not free. *Jacob* blessed his Sons, *Balaam* blessed *Israel*, these two acts being done, are both necessary upon supposition; But is was in *Jacobs* power not to have blessed his Sons, So was it not in *Balaams* power, not to have blessed *Israel*, Numb. 22. 38. *Jacobs* will was determined by himself, *Balaams* will was Physically determined by God. Therefore *Jacobs* benediction proceeded from his own free election; And *Balaams* from Gods determination. So was *Caiphas* his Prophesy, *John* 11. 51. Therefore the Text saith, *He spake not of himself*. To this *T. H.* saith nothing, but only declareth by an impertinent instance, what *Hypotheticall* signifies. And then adviseth your Lordship to take notice how Errours and Ignorance may be cloked under grave Scholastick tearmes. And I do likewise intreat your Lordship to take notice, that the greatest fraud and cheating, lurks commonly under the pretense of plain dealing; we see Juglers commonly strip up their sleeves, and promise extraordinary fair dealing before they begin to play their tricks.

Concerning the second argument drawn from the liberty of God, and the good Angells. As I cannot but approove his modesty, in suspending his judgment concerning the manner how God and the good Angells do work necessarily or freely, because he finds it not set down in the Articles of our Faith, or the Decrees of our Church, especially in this age, which is so full of Atheisme, and of those scoffers which St. *Peter* prophesied

Prophesied of, 2 *Pet.* 3. 3. Who neither believe, that there is God or Angells, or that they have a Soul, but only as salt, to keep their bodies from putrifaction; So I can by no means assent unto him, in that which followes, that is to say, that he hath proved, that Liberty and Necessity of the same kind may consist together, that is, a liberty of exercise with a necessity of exercise, or a liberty of specification, with a necessity of specification. Those actions which he saith are necessitated by passion, are for the most part dictated by reason, either truly, or apparently right, and resolved by the will it self. But it troubles him that I say, that God and the good Angells are more free than men intensively in the degree of freedom, but not extensively in the latitude of the object, according to a liberty of exercise, but not of specification, which he saith, are no distinctions, but tearmes invented to cover ignorance. Good words. Doth he onely see? Are all other men stark bling? By his favour, they are true and necessary distinctions; And if he alone do not conceive them, it is because distinctions, as all other things, have their fates, according to the capacities or prejudices of their Readers. But he urgeth two reasons, *One heate, saith he, may be more intensive than another, but not one liberty than another.* Why not, I wonder? Nothing is more proper to a man than reason, yet a man is more rationall than a child, and one man more rationall than another, that is, in respect of the use and exercise of reason. As there are degrees of understanding,

understanding, so there are of liberty. The good Angells have cleerer understandings than we, and they are not hindred with passions as we, and by consequence, they have more use of liberty than we. His second reason is, *He that can do what he will, hath all liberty, and he that cannot do what he will, hath no liberty.* If this be true, then there are no degrees of liberty indeed. But this which he calls liberty, is rather an Omnipotence than a liberty, to do whatsoever he will. A man is free to shoot, or not to shoot, although he cannot hit the white, when soever he would. We do good freely, but with more difficulty and reluctation than the good Spirits. The more rationall, and the less sensuall the will is, the greater is the degree of liberty. His other exception against liberty of exercise, and liberty of specification, is a meer mistake, which growes meerly from not rightly understanding what liberty of specification, or contrariety is. A liberty of specification, saith he, is a liberty to do, or not to do, or not to do this, or that, in particular. Upon better advice he will find, that this which he calls a liberty of specification, is a liberty of contradiction, and not of specification, nor of contrariety. To be free to do or not to do, this or that particular good, is a liberty of contradiction, so likewise to be free to do or not to do this, or that particular evill. But to be free to do both good and evill, is a liberty of contrariety, which extends to contrary objects, or to diverse kinds of things. So his reason to proove, that a liberty of exercise cannot be without

out a liberty of specification, falls flat to the ground. And he may lay aside his Lenten license for another occasion. I am ashamed to insist upon these things which are so evident, that no man can question them who doth understand them.

And here he falls into another invective against distinctions, and Scholasticall expressions, and the *Doctors of the Church, who by this means tyrannized over the understandings of other men.* What a presumption is this for one private man, who will not allow human liberty to others, to assume to himself such a license, to controll so Magistrally, and to censure of gross ignorance and tyrannising over mens judgments, yea, as causes of the troubles and tumults which are in the world, the Doctors of the Church in generall, who have flourished in all ages and all places, only for a few necessary and innocent distinctions. Truly said *Plutarch*, that a sore eye is offended with the light of the Sun; what then must the Logicians lay aside their first and second Intentions? their Abstracts and Conceits, their Subjects and Predicates, their Modes and Figures, their Method Synthetick and Analytick, their Fallacies of Composition and Division, &c? Must the morall Philosopher quitt his means and extremes, his *pricipia congenita ad acquisita*, his liberty of contradiction and contrariety, his necessity absolute and hypotheticall, &c? Must the naturall Philosopher give over his intentionall Species, his understanding Agent and Patient, his receptive

and

and eductive power of the matter, his qualities, *infinitæ* or *influxæ*, *symbolæ* or *dissymbolæ*, his temperament, *ad pondus*, and *ad justitiam*, his parts Homogeneous & Heterogeneous, his Sympathies and Antipathies, his Antiperistasis, &c? Must the Astrologer and the Geographer leave their *Apogæum* and *Perigæum*, their Arctick and Antarctick Poles, their Æquator, Zodiack, Zenith, Meridian, Horison, Zones, &c? Must the Mathematician, the Metaphysician, and the Divine, relinquish all their tearmes of Art, and proper idiotismes, because they do not rellish with *T. H.* his palate? But he will say, they are obscure expressions; What marvell is it, when the things themselves are more obscure; Let him put them into as plain English as he can, and they shall be never a whit the better understood by those who want all grounds of learning. Nothing is clearer than Mathematicall demonstration, yet let one who is altogether ignorant in Mathematicks hear it, and he will hold it to be as *T. H.* tearmes these distinctions, plain Fustian or Jargon. Every Art or Profession hath its proper mysteries and expressions, which are well known to the Sons of Art, not so to strangers. Let him consult with Military men, with Physitians, with Navigators, and he shall find this true by experience. Let him go on shipboard, and the Mariners will not leave their Sterbord and Larbord, because they please not him, or because he accounts it Gibrish. No, no, it is not the Schoole-Divines, but Innovators and seditious Oratours, who are the true causes of causes of the present troubles of Europe. *T. H.* hath forgotten what he said in his book, *De Cive cap.* 12. That it is a seditious opinion to teach, that the knowledge of good and evill belongs to private persons. And cap. 17. that in questions of Faith the Civill Magistrates ought to *consult with the Ecclesiasticall Doctors, to whom Gods blessing is derived by imposition of hands, so as not to be received in necessary truths, to whom our Saviour hath promised infallibility.* These are the very men whom he traduceth here. There he ascribes infallibility to them, here he accuseth them of gross superstitious ignorance. There he attributes too much to them, here he attributes too little. Both there and here he takes too much upon him. *The Spirits of the Prophets are subject to the Prophets*, 1 Cor. 14. 32.

J. D.

Numb. 20. Now, to the distinction it self I say first, that the proper act of liberty is election, and election is opposed, not only to coaction, but also to coarctation or determination to one. Necessitation or determination to one, may consist with spontaneity, but not with election or liberty, as hath been shewed. The very Stoicks did acknowledge a spontaneity. So our adversaries are not yet gone out of the confines of the Stoicks.

Secondly, to rip up the bottom of this business. This I take to be the clear resolution of the Schooles; There is a double act of the will, the one more remote, called *Imperatus*, that is,

in

in truth the act of some inferiour faculty, subject to the command of the will, as to open or shut ones eyes, without doubt these actions may be compelled. The other act is neerer, called *actus elicitus*, an act drawn out of the will, as to will, to choose, to elect, this may be stopped or hindered by the intervening impediment of the understanding, as a stone lying on a table is kept from its naturall motion, otherwise the will should have a kind of Omnipotence; But the will cannot be compelled to an act repugnant to its inclination, as when a stone is thrown upwards into the air, for that is both to incline, and not to incline to the same object, at the same time, which implies a contradiction. Therefore to say the will is necessitated, is to say, the will is compelled so far as the will is capable of compulsion. If a strong man holding the hand of a weaker, should therewith kill a third person, *hac quidem vis est*, this violence, the weaker did not willingly perpetrate the fact, because he was compelled. But now suppose this strong man had the will of the weaker in his power as well as the hand, and should not onely incline, but determine it secretly and insensibly to commit this act, is not the case the same? whether one ravish *Lucretia* by force, as *Tarquine*, or by amatory potions, and Magicall Incantations, not only allure her, but necessitake her to satisfy his lust, and incline her effectually, and draw her inevitably, and irresistibly to follow him spontaneously. *Lucretia* in both these conditions is to be pittied, but the latter person

person is more guilty, and deserves greater punishment, who endevours also so much as in him lies, to make *Lucretia* irresistibly partake of his crime. I dare not apply it, but thus only; Take heed how we defend those secret and invincible necessitations to evill, though spontaneous and free from coaction.

These are their fastnesses.

T. H.

IN the next place, he bringeth two arguments against distinguishing between being free from compulsion, and free from necessitation. The first is, that election is opposite, not onely to coaction or compulsion, but also to necessitation or determination to one. This is it he was to proove from the beginning, and therefore bringeth no new argument to proove it. And to those brought formerly, I have already answered; And in this place I deny again, that election is opposite to either, for when a man is compelled (for example, to subject himself to an enemy or to dy) he hath still election left in him, and a deliberation to bethink which of these two he can better endure; And he that is led to prison by force, hath election and may deliberate whether he will be hailed and trained on the ground, or make use of his feet.

Likewise when there is no compulsion, but the strength of temptation to do an evill action, being greater than the motives to abstain, necessarily determine him to the doing of it, yet he deliberates whiles sometimes the motives to do, sometimes the motives to forbear, are working on him,
and

and consequently he electeth which he will. But commonly when we see and know the strength that moves us, we acknowledge Necessity, but when we see not, or mark not the force that moves us, we then think there is none, and that it is not Causes but liberty, that produceth the action. Hence it is, that they think he does not chose this, that of necessity choseth it, but they might as well say, fire does not burn, because it burnes of necessity. The second argument is not so much an argument, as a distinction, to shew in what sense it may be said, that voluntary actions are necessitated, and in what sense not. And therefore he alledgeth as from the authority of the Schooles, and that which rippeth up the bottome of the question, that there is a double act of the will; The one he sayes, is actus Imperatus, an act done at the command of the will, by some inferiour faculty of the soul, as to open or shut ones eyes, and this act may be compelled. The other he sayes, is actus elicitus, an act allured, or an act drawn forth by allurement out of the will, as to will, to choose, to elect: This he sayes cannot be compelled. Wherein letting pass that Metaphoricall speech of attributing command and subjection to the faculties of the Soul, as if they made a Common-wealth or Family among themselves, and could speak one to another, which is very improper in searching the truth of the question. You may observe first, that to compell a voluntary act, is nothing els, but to will it, for it is all one to say, my will commands the shutting of mine eyes, or the doing of any other action, and to

say

say, I have the will to shut mine eyes. So that *actus imperatus here, might as easily have been said in English, a voluntary action, but that they that invented the tearme, understood not any thing it signified. Secondly, you may observe, that* actus elicitus, *is exemplified by these words, to Will, to Elect, to Choose, which are all one, and so to will is here made an act of the will, and indeed, as the will is a faculty, or power in a mans soul, so to will is an act of it, according to that power. But as it is absurdly said, that to dance is an act allured or drawn by fair means out of the ability to dance; so it is also to say, that to will, is an act allured or drawn out of the power to will, which power is commonly called, the Will. Howsoever it be, the summe of his distinction is, that a voluntary act may be done on compulsion, that is to say, by foul means, but to will that, or any act, cannot be but by allurement or fair means. Now, seeing fair Means, Allurements, and Enticements, produce the action which they do produce, as necessarily as threatning and foul means, it followes, that to will, may be made as necessary as any thing that is done by compulsion. So that the distinction of* actus imperatus, *and* actus elicitus, *are but words, and of no effect against necessity.*

J. D.

IN the next place follow two reasons of mine own against the same distinction, the one taken from the former grounds, that Election cannot consist with determination to one. To this (he saith) he hath *answered already.* No,

truth

Truth is founded upon a Rock. He hath been so far from prevailing against it, that he hath not been able to shake it. Now again, he tells us, that *Election is not opposite to either*, (Necessitation or Compulsion) He might even as well tell us, that a stone thrown upwards mooves naturally; Or, that a woman can be ravished with her own will. Consent takes away the Rape. This is the strangest liberty that ever was heard of, that a man is compelled to do what he would not, and yet is free to do what he will. And this he tells us upon the old score, that *he, who submits to his enemy for fear of death, chooseth to submit.* But we have seen formerly, that this, which he calls compulsion, is not compulsion properly, nor that naturall determination of the will, to one which is opposite to true Liberty. He who submits to an enemy for saving his life, doth either onely counterfeit, and then there is no will to submit, this disguise is no more than a stepping aside, to avoid a present blow, Or els he doth sincerely will a submission, and then the will is changed; There is a vast difference between compelling and changing the will. Either God or man may change the will of man, either by varying the condition of things, or by informing the party otherwise, but compelled it cannot be, that is, it cannot both will this, and not will this, as it is invested with the same circumstances, though, if the act were otherwise circumstantiated, it might nill that freely, which now it wills freely. Wherefore the kind of actions are called mixt

actions

actions, that is partly voluntary, partly unvoluntary. That which is compelled is a mans present condition or distress, that is not voluntary nor chosen. That which is chosen, is the remedy of its distress, that is voluntary. So hypothetically supposing a man were not in that distress they are involuntary, but absolutely without any supposition at all, taking the case as it is, they are voluntary. His other instance of *a man forced to prison, that he may choose whether he will be haled thither upon the ground, or walk upon his feet* is not true. By his leave, that is not as he pleaseth, but as it pleaseth them who have him in their power. If they will drag him, he is not free to walk; And if they give him leave to walk, he is not forced to be dragged. Having laid this foundation, he begins to build upon it, that *other passions do necessitate as much as fear*; But he erres doubly; first, in his foundation, fear doth not determine the rationall will naturally and necessarily; The last and greatest of the five terrible things is death, yet the fear of death cannot necessitate a resolved mind to do a dishonest action, which is worse than death. The fear of the fiery furnace could not compell the three Children to worship an Idoll, nor the fear of the Lions necessitate *Daniel*, to omit his duty to God, It is our frailty, that we are more afraid of empty shadows than of substantiall dangers, because they are neerer our senses, as little Children fear a Mouse or a Visard, more than fire or weather. But as a fitte of the stone takes away the sense of the gout for the present, so the greater passion doth extinguish the less. The fear of Gods wrath, and eternall torments doth expell corporall fear, *fear not them who kill the body, but fear him who is able to cast both body and soul into hell.* Luk. 7. 4. *Da veniam Imperator, tu carcerem, ille gehennam minatur*, Excuse me, O Emperor, thou threatens men with prison, but he threatens me with hell. Secondly, he erres in his superstruction also. There is a great difference, as to this case of justifying, or not justifying an action between force and fear, and other passions; Force doth not only lessen the sin, but takes it quite away, *Deut*. 22. 26. He who forced a betrothed Damsell was to die; *but unto the Damsell* (saith he) *thou shalt do nothing, there is in her no fault worthy of death. Tamars* beauty, or *Ammons* love did not render him innocent, but *Ammons* force rendred *Tamar* innocent. But fear is not so prevalent as force. Indeed if fear be great, and justly grounded, such as may fall upon a constant man, though it do not dispense with the transgression of the negative Precepts of God or Nature, because they bind to all-times, yet it diminisheth the offence, even against them, and pleads for pardon. But it dispenseth in many cases with the transgression of the positive Law, either Divine or humane; Because it is not probable, that God or the Law, would oblige man to the observation of all positive Precepts, with so great dammage as the loss of his life. The omission of Circumcision was no sin, whilest the *Israelites* were travelling through the wildernesse. By *T. H.* his permission, I will propose

propose a case to him. A Gentleman sends his servant with mony to buy his dinner, some Ruffians meet him by the way, and take it from him by force, The servant cryed for help, and did what he could to defend himself, but all would not serve. The servant is innocent, if he was to be tried before a Court of Areopagites. Or suppose the Ruffians did not take it from him by force, but drew their swords and threatned to kill him, except he delivered it himself; no wise man will conceive, that it was either the Masters intention, or the servants duty, to hazard his life, or his limbes, for saving of such a trifling sum. But on the other side suppose this servant, passing by some Cabaret, or Tennis-court, where his Camerads were drinking or playing, should stay with them, and drink or play away his mony, and afterwards plead as *T. H.* doth here, that he was overcome by the meer strength of temptation, I trow, neither *T. H.* nor any man els would admit of this excuse, but punish him for it, because, neither was he necessitated by the temptation, and what strength it had, was by his own fault, in respect of that vitious habit which he had contracted of drinking or gaming, Jam. 1, 14. *Every man is tempted when he is drawn away of his own lust and entised.* Disordered passions of anger, hatred, lust, if they be consequent (as the case is here put by *T. H.*) and flow from deliberation and election, they do not only not diminish the fault, but they aggravate it, and render it much greater.

He talks much of *the motives to do, and the motives*

motives to forbear, how they work upon and determine a man, as if a reasonable man were no more than a Tennis-ball, to be tossed to and fro by the Racketts of the second causes; As if the will had no power to moove it self, but were meerly passive, like an artificiall Popingay remooved hither and thither by the bolts of the Archers, who shoot on this side and on that. What are motives but reasons or discourses framed by the understanding, and freely mooved by the will? What, are the will and the understanding but faculties of the same soul? and what is liberty but a power resulting from them both? To say that the will is determined by these motives, is as much as to say, that the Agent is determined by himself; If there be no necessitation before the judgment of right reason doth dictate to the will, then there is no antecedent, no extrinsecall necessitation at all. All the world knowes, that when the Agent is determined by himself, then the effect is determined likewise in its cause. But if he determined himself freely, then the effect is free. Motives determine not naturally but morally, which kind of determination may consist with true liberty. But if *T. H.* his opinion were true, that the will were naturally determined by the Physicall and speciall influence of extrinsecall causes, not onely motives were vain, but reason it self, and deliberation were vain. No, saith he, they are not vain, because they are the means. Yes, if the means be superfluous they are vain, what needed such a circuit of deliberation to advise what is

fit

fit to be done, when it is already determined extrinsecally, what must be done.

He saith, that *the ignorance of the true causes, and their power is the reason, why we ascribe the effect to liberty, but when we seriously consider the causes of things, we acknowledge a necessity.* No such thing, but just the contrary. The more we consider, and the cleerer we understand, the greater is the liberty, and the more the knowledge of our own liberty. The less we consider, and the more incapable that the understanding is, the lesser is the liberty, and the knowledge of it. And where there is no consideration, nor use of reason, there is no liberty at all, there is neither morall good nor evill. Some men, by reason that their exteriour senses are not totally bound, have a trick to walk in their sleep. Suppose such an one in that case should cast himself down a pair of staires, or from a bridge, and break his neck, or drown himself, it were a mad Jury that would find this man accessary to his own death. Why? because it was not freely done, he had not then the use of reason.

Lastly, he tells us, that *the will doth choose of necessity, as well as the fire burnes of necessity.* If he intend no more but this, that election is the proper and naturall act of the will, as burning is of the fire, or that the elective power is as necessarily in a man as visibility; he speaks truly, but most impertinently; For, the question is not now of the elective power, *in actu primo*, whether it be an essentiall faculty of the soul, but whether the act of electing this or that particular

particular object be free, & undetermined by any antecedent and extrinsecall causes. But if he intend it in this other sense, that as the fire hath no power to suspend its burning, nor to distinguish between those combustible matters which are put unto it, but burnes that which is put unto it necessarily, if it be combustible: So the will hath no power to refuse that which it wills, nor to suspend its own appetite. He erres grossely. The will hath power, either to will or nill, or to suspend, that is neither to will nor nill the same object; Yet even the burning of the fire, if it be considered as it is invested with all particular circumstances, is not otherwise so necessary an action as *T. H.* imagineth. Two things are required to make an effect necessary. First, that it be produced by a necessary cause, such as fire is; Secondly, that it be necessarily produced. *Protagoras* an Atheist, began his Book thus. *Concerning the gods, I have nothing to say, whether they be, or they be not*, for which his Book was condemned by the *Athenians* to be burned. The fire was a necessary agent, but the sentence or the application of the fire to the Book, was a free act, and therefore the burning of his Book was free. Much more the rationall will is free, which is both a voluntary agent, and acts voluntarily.

My second reason against this distinction of Liberty from Compulsion, but not from necessitation is new, and demonstrates cleerly, that to necessitate the will, by a Physicall necessity, is to compell the will so far as the will is capable of

Com-

Compulsion, and that he, who doth necessitate the will to evill, after that manner is the true cause of evill, and ought rather to be blamed than the will it self. But *T. H.* for all he saith he is not surprised, can be contented upon better advise to steal by all this in silence; And to hide this tergiversation from the eyes of the Reader, he makes an empty shew of braving against that famous and most necessary distinction between the *elicite* and *imperate* acts of the will; first, because the termes are *improper*; secondly, because they are *obscure*. What Triviall and Grammaticall objections are these, to be used against the universall currant of Divines and Philosophers. *Verborum ut nummorum*, It is in words, as it is in mony. Use makes them proper and currant, A *Tyrant* at first, signified a lawfull and just Prince; Now, use hath quite changed the sense of it, to denote either an Usurper, or an Oppressor. The word *præmunire* is now grown a good word in our English Lawes by use and tract of time; And yet at first it was meerly mistaken for a *præmonere*. The names of Sunday, Munday, Tuesday, were derived at first from those Heathenish Deities, the Sun, the Moon, and the warlike God of the Germans. Now we use them for distinction sake onely, without any relation to their first originall. He is too froward that will refuse a piece of coin that is currant throughout the world, because it is not stamped after his own fancy. So is he that rejects a good word, because he understands not the derivation of it. We see forreine words are

daily

daily naturalized, and made free Denizons in every Country. But why are the tearmes improper? Becaufe, faith he, *It attributes command, and fubjection to the faculties of the foul, as if they made a Common-wealth or family among themfelves, and could fpeak one to another,* Therefore he faith, *they who invented this tearm of* Actus Imperatus, *underftood not any thing what it fignified.* No, why not? It feemeth to me they underftood it better than thofe who except againft it. They knew, there are *mentall tearmes*, which are onely conceived in the mind, as well as *vocall tearmes*, which are expreffed with the tongue. They knew that howfoever a Superiour do intimate a direction to his inferiour, it is ftill a command. *Tarquin* commanded his fon, by onely ftriking off the topps of the Poppies, and was by him both underftood and obeyed. Though there be no formall *Common-wealth* or *family* either in the body, or in the foul of man, yet there is a fubordination in the body, of the inferiour members to the head, there is a fubordination in the foul of the inferiour faculties to the rationall will. Far be it from a reafonable man, fo far to difhonour his own nature, as to equall fancy with underftanding, or the fenfitive appetite with the reafonable will. A power of command there is without all queftion, though there be fome doubt in what faculty this command doth principally refide, whether in the will or in the underftanding. The true refolution is, that the directive command for counfel is in the underftanding; And the applicative command,

mand, or empire, for putting in execution of what is directed, is in the will. The same answer serves for his second impropriety, about the word Elicite. For, saith he, *as it is absurdly said, that to dance, is an act allured, or drawn by fair means out of the ability to dance; So it is absurdly said, that to will or choose, is an act drawn out of the power to will.* His objection is yet more improper than their expression. The art of dancing rather resembles the understanding, than the will. That drawing, which the Schools intend, is cleer of another nature, from that which he conceives; By *elicitation*, he understands, a perswading or enticing with flattering words, or sweet alluring insinuations, to choose, this or that. But that *elicitation*, which the Schools intend, is a deducing of the power of the will into act, that *drawing*, which they mention, is meerly from the appetibility of the object, or of the end, as a man *drawes* a Child after him with the sight of a fair Apple, or a Shepheard *drawes* his sheep after him with the sight of a green bough: So the end *drawes* the will to it, by a Metaphoricall motion. What he understands here by an ability to dance, is more than I know, or any man els, untill he express himself in more proper tearmes, whether he understand the *locomotive* faculty alone, or the art, or acquired habit of dancing alone, or both of these jointly. It may be said aptly without any absurdity, that the act of dancing is drawn out (*elicitur*) of the *locomotive* faculty helped by the acquired habit. He who is so scrupulous about the received

phrases

phrases of the Schools should not have let so many improper expressions have dropped from his pen; as in this very passage he confounds the *compelling of a voluntary action*, with the commanding of a voluntary action, and *willing* with *electing*, which he saith, *are all one*. Yet to will properly respects the end, to elect the means.

His other objection against this distinction of the acts of the will into Elicite and Imperate, is obscurity. *Might it not* (saith he) *have been as easily said in English, a voluntary action.* Yes, it might have been said as easily, but not as truly, nor properly. Whatsoever hath its originall from the will, whether immediatly or mediatly, whether it be a proper act of the will it self, as to elect, or an act of the understanding, as to deliberate, or an act of the inferiour faculties, or of the members, is a voluntary action, but neither the act of reason nor of the senses, nor of the sensitive appetite, nor of the members are the poper acts of the will, nor drawn immediatly out of the will it self, but the members and faculties are applyed to their proper and respective acts by the power of the will.

And so he comes to cast up the totall sum of my second reason, with the same faith, that the unjust Steward did make his accounts, Luk. 16. *The sum of* J. D.'s *distinction is* (saith he) *that a voluntary act may be done on compulsion* (just contrary to what I have maintained) *that is to say, by foul means. But to will that, or any act cannot be but by allurement or fair means.* I confess fefs the diſtinction is mine, becauſe I uſe it, as the Sun is mine, or the Air is mine, that is common to me, with all who treat of this ſubject. But his miſtakes are ſo thick, both in relating my mind, and his own, that the Reader may conclude, he is wandered out of his known way. I will do my duty to ſhew him the right way. Firſt, no acts, which are properly ſaid to be compelled, are voluntary. Secondly, acts of terrour (which he calls foul means) which are ſometimes in a large improper ſenſe called compulſory actions, may be, and for the moſt part are conſiſtent with true liberty. Thirdly, actions proceeding from blandiſhments or ſweet perſuaſions (which he calls fair means) if they be indeliberated as in children, who want the uſe of reaſon, are not preſently free actions. Laſtly, the ſtrength of conſequent, and deliberated deſires doth neither diminiſh guilt, nor excuſe from puniſhment, as juſt fears of extreme and imminent dangers threatned by extrinſecall agents often do, becauſe the ſtrength of the former proceeds from our own fault, and was freely elected in the cauſes of it; But neither deſires nor fears, which are conſequent and deliberated, do abſolutely neceſſitate the will.

J. D.

Numb. 21. THE reſt are umbrages quickly diſpelled, firſt, the Aſtrologer ſteps up, and ſubjects Liberty to the motions of Heaven, to the aſpects and aſcenſions of the Starrs, -- *Plus etenim fati valet hora benigni.* (*Marti.*
Quam ſi nos Veneris commendet epiſtola

I stand not much upon them who cannot see the fishes swimming besides them in the rivers, yet believe they see those which are in heaven. Who promise great treasures to others, and beg a groat for themselves. The Starrs at the most, do but incline, they cannot necessitate.

Secondly, the Physitian subjects liberty to the complexion and temperature of the body. But yet this comes not home to a necessity. *Socrates*, and many others by assiduous care have corrected the pernicious propensions, which flowed from their temperatures.

T. H.

IN the rest of his discourse he reckoneth up the opinions of certain professions of men, touching the causes, wherein the necessity of things, which they maintain, consisteth. And first he saith, the Astrologer deriveth his necessity from the Starrs. Secondly, that the Physician attributeth it to the temper of the body. For my part, I am not of their opinion, because neither the Starrs alone, nor the temperature of the Patient alone is able to produce any effect without the concurrence of all other agents. For, there is hardly any one action, how casuall soever it seem, to the causing whereof concur not whatsoever is in rerum natura. Which because it is a great Paradox, and depends on many antecedent speculations I do not press in this place.

J. D.

J. D.

TOwards the later end of my discourse I answered some specious pretences against liberty, The two first were of the Astrologer and the Physician. The one subjecting liberty to the motions and influences of the heavenly bodies; The other to the complexions of men. The sum of my answer was, that the Starrs and complexions do incline, but not at all necessitate the will. To which all judicious Astronomers and Physicians do assent. And *T. H.* himself doth not dissent from it. So as to this part there needs no reply.

But whereas he mentions a *great paradox of his own, that there is hardly any one action to the causing of which concurres not whatsoever is in rerum natura*, I can but smile to see with what ambition our great undertakers do affect to be accounted, the first founders of strange opinions, as if the devising of an ill grounded Paradox were as great an honour as the invention of the needle, or the discovery of the new world. And to this Paradox in Particular, I meddle not with naturall actions, because the subject of my discourse is morall liberty; But if he intend not only the kinds of things, but every individuall creature, and not onely in naturall but voluntary actions, I desire to know how *Prester John*, or the great *Mogol*, or the King of *China*, or any one of so many millions of their subjects do concur to my writing of this reply. If they do not among his other speculations, concerning this matter, I hope he will give us some restrictions,

restrictions. It were hard to make all the *Negroes* accessary to all the murthers that are committed in Europe.

J. D.

THirdly, the morall Philosopher tells us how Numb. 22. we are haled hither and thither with outward objects. To this I answer,

First, that the power, which outward objects have over us, is for the most part by our own default, because of those vitious habits which we have contracted. Therefore, though the actions seem to have a kind of violence in them, yet they were free and voluntary in their first originalls. As a paralitick man, to use *Aristotles* comparison, shedding the liquor deserves to be punished, for though his act be unwilling, yet his intemperance was willing, whereby he contracted this infirmity.

Secondly, I answer, that concupiscence, and custome, and bad company, and outward objects do indeed make a proclivity, but not a necessity. By Prayers, Tears, Meditations, Vowes, Watchings, Fastings, Humi-cubations a man may get a contrary habit, and gain the victory, not onely over outward objects, but also over his own corruptions, and become the King of the little world of himself.

Si metuis, si prava cupis, si duceris irâ,
Servitii patiere jugum, tolerabis iniquas
Interius leges. Tunc omnia jure tenebis,
Cum poteris rex esse tui.

Thirdly, a resolved mind, which weighs all things

things judiciously, and provides for all occurrences, is not so easily surprised with outward objects. Onely *Ulysses* wept not at the meeting with his wife and son. I would beat thee (said the Philosopher) but that I am angry. One spake lowest when he was most mooved. Another poured out the water when he was thirsty. Another made a Covenant with his eyes. Neither opportunity nor entisement could prevail with *Joseph*. Nor the Musick, nor the fire with the three Children. It is not the strength of the wind, but the lightness of the chaff, which causeth it to be blown away. Outward objects do not impose a morall, much less a Physicall necessity, they may be dangerous, but cannot be destructive to true liberty.

T. H.

Thirdly, he disputeth against the opinion of them that say, externall objects presented to men of such and such temperatures, do make their actions necessary. And sayes, the power that such objects have over us, proceed from our own fault; But that is nothing to the purpose, if such fault of ours proceedeth from causes, not in our own power. And therefore that opinion may hold true for all this answer: Further he saith, Prayer, Fasting, &c. may alter our habits. 'Tis true, but when they do so, they are causes of the contrary habit, and make it necessary; As the former habit had been necessary, if Prayer, Fasting, &c. had not been. Besides we are not mooved, nor disposed to prayer, or any other action but by outward objects, as pious company, godly preachers, or something equivalent. Thirdly, he saith, a resolved mind is not easily surprised. As the mind of Ulysses, who when others wept, he alone wept not. And of the Philosopher that abstained from striking, because he found himself angry. And of him that poured out the water when he was thirsty; And the like; Such things I confess have, or may have been done, and do prove onely that it was not necessary for Ulysses then to weep, nor for the Philosopher to strike, nor for that other man to drink, but it does not prove that it was not necessary for Ulysses then to abstaine, as he did from weeping, nor the Philosopher to abstain as he did from striking; Nor the other man to forbear drinking. And yet that was the thing he ought to have proved.

Lastly, he confesseth, that the disposition of objects may be dangerous to liberty, but cannot be destructive. To which I answer 'tis impossible; For, liberty is never in any other danger than to be lost: And if it cannot be lost, which he confesseth, I may infer it can be in no danger at all.

J. D.

THe third pretense was out of morall Philophy misunderstood, that outward objects do necessitate the will. I shall not need to repeat what he hath omitted, but onely to satisfie his exceptions; The first is, that it is not materiall, *though the power of outward objects do proceed from our own faults, if such faults of our proceed not from causes in our own power.* Well, but what if they do proceed from causes that are in our own power, as in truth they do, then his answer is a

meere

meere subterfuge. If our faults proceed from causes that are not, and were not in our own power, then they are not our faults at all. It is not a fault in us not to do those things, which never were in our power to do. But they are the faults of these causes from whence they do proceed. Next he confesseth, that it is in our power by good endeavours, to alter those vitious habits which we had contracted, and to get the contrary habit. *True (saith he) but then the contrary habit doth necessitate the one way, as well as the former habit did the other way.* By which very consideration it appeares, that that which he calls a necessity is no more but a proclivity. If it were a true necessity, it could not be avoided, nor altered by our endeavours. The truth is Acquired habits do help and assist the faculty; but they do not necessitate the faculty. He who hath gotten to himself an habit of temperance, may yet upon occasion commit an intemperate act. And so on the contrary. Acts are not opposed to habits, but other habits. He addes, *that we are not mooved to prayer or any other action but by outward objects, as pious company, godly Preachers, or something equivalent.* Wherein are two other mistakes, first, to make godly Preachers, and pious company, to be outward *objects*, which are outward *Agents*. Secondly, to affirm that the will is not moved but by outward objects. The will is mooved by it self, by the understanding, by the sensitive passions, by Angells good and bad, by men, and most effectually by acts or habits infused by God, whereby by the will is excited extraordinarily indeed, but efficaciously and determinately. This is more than equivalent with outward objects.

Another branch of mine answer was, that a resolved and prepared mind is able to resist both, the appetibility of objects, and the unruliness of passions. As I shewed by examples. He answers that I prove *Ulysses* was not necessitated to weep, nor the Philosopher to strike, but I do not prove that they were not necessitated to forbear. He saith true. I am not now proving, but answering. Yet my answer doth sufficiently prove that which I intend. That the rationall will hath power, both to sleight the most appetible objects, and to controll the most unruly passions. When he hath given a clear solution to those proofs which I have produced, then it will be time for him to cry for more work.

Lastly, whereas I say, that outward objects may be dangerous, but cannot be destructive to true liberty. He catcheth at it, and objects that *liberty is in no danger, but to be lost, but I say, it cannot be lost, therefore* (he infers) *that it is in no danger at all.* I answer; First, that liberty is in more danger to be abused than to be lost. Many more men do abuse their wits than lose them. Secondly, liberty is in danger likewise to be weakened or diminished, as when it is clogged by vitious habits contracted by our selves, and yet it is not totally lost. Thirdly, though liberty cannot be totally lost out of the world, yet it may be totally lost to this or that particular man, as to the exercise of it. Reason is the root

root of liberty, and though nothing be more naturall to a man than reason, yet many by excess of study, or by continuall gurmandizing, or by some extravagant passion, which they have cherished in themselves, or by doting too much upon some affected object, do become very sotts, and deprive themselves of the use of reason, and consequently of Liberty. And when the benefit of liberty is not thus universally lost, yet it may be lost respectively to this or that particular occasion. As he who makes choise of a bad wife, hath lost his former liberty to chose a good one.

J. D.

Numb. 23. Fourthly, the naturall Philosopher doth teach, that the will doth necessarily follow the last dictate of the understanding. It is true indeed the will should follow the direction of the understanding, but I am not satisfied that it doth evermore follow it. Sometimes this saying hath place, *Video meliora proboq; Deteriora sequor.* As that great Roman said of two Sailers, that the one produced the better reasons, but the other must have the office. So reason often lies dejected at the feet of affection, Things neerer to the senses moove more powerfully. Do what a man can, he shall sorrow more for the death of his child, than for the sin of his soul. Yet appreciatively in the estimation of judgment, he accounts the offence of God, a greater evill than any temporall loss.

Next, I do not believe that a man is bound to weigh the expedience or inexpedience of every

every ordinary triviall action to the least grain in the ballance of his understanding, or to run up into his Watch-Tower with his perspective to take notice of every Jack-daw that flies by, for fear of some hidden danger. This seemes to me to be a prostitution of reason to petite observations, as concerning every rag that a man weares, each drop of drink, each morsell of bread that he eates, each pace that he walks. Thus many stepps must he go, not one more, nor one less, under pain of mortall sin. What is this but a Rack and a Gibbet to the Conscience? But God leaves many things indifferent, though man be so curious he will not. A good Architect will be sure to provide sufficient materialls for his building, but what particular number of stones, or trees, he troubles not his head. And suppose he should weigh each action thus, yet he doth not, so still there is liberty. Thirdly, I conceive it is possible in this mist and weakness of human apprehension, for two actions to be so equally circumstantiated, that no discernible difference can appear between them upon discussion. As suppose a Chirurgion should give two plaisters to his Patient, and bid him apply either of them to his wound, what can induce his reason more to the one than to the other, but that he may refer it to chance, whether he will use? But leaving these probable speculations which I submit to better judgments, I answer the Philosopher briefly thus; Admitting that the will did necessarily follow the last dictate of the understanding as certainly in many things it doth. Yet,

First

First, this is no extrinsecall determination from without, and a mans own resolution is not destructive to his own liberty, but depends upon it. So the person is still free.

Secondly, this determination is not antecedent, but joyned with the action. The understanding and the will, are not different Agents, but distinct faculties of the same soul: Here is an infallibility, or an hypotheticall necessity, as we say, *Quicquid est quando est, necesse est esse*: A necessity of consequence, but not a necessity of consequent. Though an Agent have certainly determined, and so the action be become infallible, yet if the Agent did determine freely, the action likewise is free.

T. H.

THE fourth opinion which he rejecteth, is of them that make the will necessarily to follow the last dictate of the understanding, but it seems he understands, that Tenet in another sense than I do. For he speaketh as if they that held it did suppose men must dispute the sequell of every action they do, great & small, to the least grain, which is a thing, that he thinks with reason to be untrue. But I understand it to signifie, that the will followes the last opinion or judgment, immediatly preceding the action, concerning whether it be good to do it or not, whether he hath weighed it long before or not all. And that I take to be the meaning of them that hold it. As for example, when a man strikes, his will to strike followes necessarily that thought he had of the sequell of his stroke immediately before the lifting of his hand. Now if it be understood in that sense, the last dictate of the understanding does certainly necessitate the action, though not as the whole cause, yet as the last cause, as the last feather necessitates the breaking of an horses-back, when there are so many laid on before, as there needeth but the addition of that one to make the weight sufficient. That which he alledgeth against this, is first, out of a Poet, who in the person of Medæa *sayes*, Video Meliora proboque, Deteriora sequor. *But the saying (as pretty as it is) is not true, for though* Medæa *saw many reasons to forbear killing her children, yet the last dictate of her judgment was, that the present revenge of her husband outweighed them all. And thereupon that wicked action followed necessarily. Then the story of the* Romans, *that of two competitors said, one had the better reasons, but the other must have the office. This also maketh against him, for the last dictate of his judgment, that had the bestowing of the office was this, that it was better to take a great bribe, than reward a great merit. Thirdly, he objects that things neerer the senses moove more powerfully than reason. What followeth thence but this, That the sense of the present good is commonly more immediate to the Action, than the foresight of the evill consequents to come. Fourthly, whereas he sayes, that do what a man can, he shall sorrow more for the death of his son, than for the sin of his soul; it makes nothing to the last dictate of the understanding, but it argues plainly, that sorrow for sin is not voluntary. And by consequence repentance proceedeth from causes.*

J. D.

J. D.

THE fourth pretense alledged against Liberty was, that the will doth necessarily follow the last dictate of the understanding, This objection is largely answered before in severall places of this Reply, and particularly, *Numb.* 7. In my former discourse, I gave two answers to it: The one certain and undoubted, That supposing the last dictate of the understanding did alwayes determine the will, yet this determination being not antecedent in time, nor proceeding from extrinsecall causes, but from the proper resolution of the Agent, who had now freely determined himself, it makes no absolute necessity, but onely hypotheticall, upon supposition that the Agent hath determined his own will, after this or that manner. Which being the main answer, *T. H.* is so farr from taking it away, that he takes no notice of it. The other part of mine answer was probable; That it is not alwayes certain, that the will doth alwayes actually follow the last dictate of the understanding, though it alwayes ought to follow it. Of which I gave then three reasons, one was, that actions may be so equally circumstantiated, or the case so intricate, that reason cannot give a positive sentence, but leaves the election to liberty or chance. To this he answers not a word. Another of my reasons was, because reason doth not weigh, nor is bound to weigh the convenience or inconvenience of every individuall action to the uttermost grain in the balance of true judgement, The truth of this reason is confessed by *T. H.*

though

though he might have had more abetters in this than in the most part of his discourse, that nothing is indifferent, that a man cannot streak his beard on one side, but it was either necessary to do it, or sinfull to omit it, from which confession of his, it followes, that in all those actions, wherein reason doth not define what is most convenient, there the will is free from the determination of the understanding. And by consequence the last feather is wanting to break the horses back; A third reason was, because passions and affections sometimes prevail against judgment, as I prooved by the example of *Medæa* and *Cæsar*, by the neerness of the objects to the senses, and by the estimation of a temporall loss more than sin. Against this reason, his whole answer is addressed. And first, he explaneth the sense of the assertion by the comparison of the last feather, wherewith he seems to be delighted, seeing he useth it now the second time. But let him like it as he will, it is improper for three reasons; First, the determination of the judgment is no part of the weight, but is the sentence of the trier. The understanding weigheth all Things, Objects, Means, Circumstances, Convenience, Inconvenience, but it self is not weighed. Secondly, the sensitive passion in in some extraordinary cases, may give a counterfeit weight to the object, if it can detein or divert reason from the ballance, but ordinarily the Means, Circumstances, and Causes concurrent they have their whole weight from the understanding. So as they do not press the horses

back

back at all untill reason lay them on. Thirdly, he conceives that as each feather hath a certain naturall weight, whereby it concurres not arbitrarily, but necessarily towards the overcharging of the horse ; So all objects and causes have a naturall efficiency whereby they do Physically determin the will, which is a great mistake. His Objects, his Agents, his Motives, his Passions, and all his concurrent causes, ordinarily do onely moove the will morally, not determine it naturally. So as it hath in all ordinary actions a free dominion over it self.

His other example of a man that strikes, *whose will to strike followeth necessarily that thought he had of the sequell of his stroke immediately before the lifting up of his hand)* as it confounds passionate, indeliberate thoughts, with the dictates of right reason. So it is very uncertain, for between the cup and the lipps, between the lifting up of the hand, and the blow, the will may alter, and the judgment also. And lastly, it is impertinent, for that necessity of striking proceeds from the free determination of the Agent, and not from the speciall influence of any outward determining causes. And so it is onely a necessity upon supposition.

Concerning *Medæas* choise, the strength of the argument doth not lye either in the fact of *Medæa*, which is but a fiction, or in the authority of the Poet, who writes things rather to be admired than believed, but in the experience of all men, who find it to be true in themselves.

That

That sometimes reason doth shew unto a man the exorbitancy of his passion, that what he desires is but a pleasant good, that what he loseth by such a choise is an honest good, That that which is honest is to be preferred before that which is pleasant, yet the will pursues that which is pleasant, and neglects that which is honest. St. *Paul* saith as much in earnest as is feined of *Medæa*. That *he approoved not that which he did, and* that *he did that which he hated*, Rom. 7. 15. The Roman Story is mistaken; There was no bribe in the case but affection. Whereas I urge that those things, which are neerer to the senses do moove more powerfully, he layes hold on it; and without answering to that for which I produced it, infers, *That the sense of present good is more immediate to the action than the foresight of evill consequents.* Which is true, but it is not absolutely true by any antecedent necessity. Let a man do what he may do, and what he ought to do, and sensitive objects will lose that power which they have by his own fault, and neglect. Antecedent or indeliberate concupiscence doth sometimes (but rarely) surprise a man, and render the action not free. But consequent and deliberated concupiscence, which proceeds from the rationall will doth render the action more free, not less free; and introduceth onely a necessity upon supposition.

Lastly, he saith, that *a mans mourning more for the loss of his Child than for his sin, makes nothing to the last dictate of the understanding.*

Yes

Yes, very much. Reason dictates, that a sin committed, is a greater evill than the loss of a child, and ought more to be lamented for, yet we see daily how affection prevailes against the dictate of reason; That which he inferrs from hence, that *sorrow for sin is not voluntary, and by consequence that repentance proceedeth from causes*, is true, as to the latter part of it, but not in his sense. The causes from whence repentance doth proceed are Gods grace preventing, and mans will concurring. God prevents freely, man concurs freely. Those inferiour Agents, which sometimes do concur as subordinate to the grace of God, do not, cannot, determine the will naturally. And therefore the former part of his inference, that sorrow for sin is not voluntary, is untrue, and altogether groundless. That is much more truly, and much more properly said to be voluntary, which proceeds from judgment, and from the rationall will, than that which proceeds from passion, and from the sensitive will. One of the main grounds of all *T. H.* his errours in this question is, that he acknowledgeth no efficacy, but that which is naturall. Hence is this wild consequence, *Repentance hath causes*, and therefore *it is not voluntary*. Free effects have free causes, necessary effects necessary causes, voluntary effects have sometimes free, sometimes necessary causes.

J. D.

J. D.

Fiftly, and lastly, the Divine labours to find out a way how liberty may consist with the prescience and decrees of God. But of this I had not very long since occasion to write a full discourse, in answer to a Treatise against the prescience of things contingent. I shall for the present only repeat these two things. First, we ought not to desert a certain truth, because we are not able to comprehend the certain manner. God should be but a poor God, if we were able perfectly to comprehend all his Actions and Attributes.

Secondly, in my poor judgment, which I ever do & ever shall submit to better, the readiest way to reconcile Contingence and Liberty, with the decrees and prescience of God, and most remote from the altercations of these times, is to subject future cōtingents to the aspect of God, according to that presentiallity which they have in eternity. Not that things future, which are not yet existent & coexistent with God, but because the infinite knowledge of God, incircling all times in the point of eternity, doth attain to their future Being, from whence proceeds their objective and intelligible Being. The main impediment which keeps men from subscribing to this way is, because they conceive eternity to be an everlasting succession, and not one indivisible point. But if they consider, that whatsoever is in God is God, That there are no accidents in him, for that which is infinitely perfect cannot be further perfected, That as God is not wise but Wisdom

Numb. 24.

it self, not just but Justice it self, so he is not eternall but Eternity it self. They must needs conclude that therefore this eternity is indivisible, because God is indivisible, and therefore not successive, but altogether an infinite point, comprehending all times within it self.

T. H.

THE last part of this discourse conteineth his opinion about reconciling Liberty with the Prescience, and Decrees of God, otherwise than some Divines have done, against whom he had formerly written a Treatise, out of which he only repeateth two things. One is, that we ought not to desert a certain truth, for not being able to comprehend the certain manner of it. And I say the same, as for example, that he ought not to desert this certain truth; That there are certain and necessary causes, which make every man to will what he willeth, though he do not yet conceive in what manner the will of man is caused. And yet I think the manner of it, is not very hard to conceive, seeing that we see daily, that praise, dispraise, reward, punishment, good and evill, sequells of mens actions retained in memory, do frame and make us to the election of whatsoever it be that we elect. And that the memory of such things proceeds from the senses. And sense from the operation of the objects of sense, which are externall to us, and governed onely by God Almighty. And by consequence, all actions, even of free and voluntary Agents are necessary.

The other thing he repeateth is, that the best way to reconcile Contingency and Liberty, with the

the prescience and decrees of God, is to subject future contingents to the aspect of God. The same is also my opinion, but contrary to what he hath all this while laboured to prove. For, hitherto he held liberty and necessity, that is to say, liberty and the decrees of God irreconcilable, unless the aspect of God (which word appeareth now the first time in this discourse) signifie somewhat els besides Gods will and decree, which I cannot understand. But he adds, that we must subject them according to that presentiality which they have in eternity, which he sayes cannot be done by them that conceive eternity to be an everlasting succession, but onely by them that conceive it an indivisible point. To this I answer, that as soon as I can conceive Eternity an indivisible point, or any thing, but an everlasting succession, I will renounce all I have written in this subject. I know St. Thomas Aquinas *calls eternity* Nunc stans, *an ever abiding now, which is easy enough to say, but though I fain would, I never could conceive it. They that can, are more happy than I. But in the mean time he alloweth hereby all men to be of my opinion, save onely those that conceive in their minds a* nunc stans, *which I think are none. I understand as little how it can be true that God is not just, but Justice it self, not wise but Wisedom it self, not eternall but Eternity it self. Nor how he concludes thence, that Eternity is a ponit indivisible, and not a succession. Nor in what sense it can be said, that an infinite point, &c. wherein is no succession, can comprehend all times, though time be successive.*

These

These phrases I find not in the Scripture. I wonder therefore, what was the designe of the School-men, to bring them up, unless they thought a man could not be a true Christian, unless his understanding be first strangled with such hard sayings.

And thus much in answer to his discourse, wherein I think not onely his squadrons, but also his reserves of distinctions are defeated. And now your Lordship shall have my doctrine concerning the same question, with my reasons for it positively and briefly as I can, without any tearmes of Art in plain English.

J. D.

THat poor discourse which I mention, was not written against any Divines, but in way of examination of a French Treatise, which your Lordships Brother did me the honour to shew me at *York*; My assertion is most true, that we ought not to desert a certain truth, because we are not able to comprehend the certain manner. Such a truth is that which I maintain, that the will of man in ordinary actions is free from extrinsecall determination. A truth demonstrable in reason, received and believed by all the world. And therefore though I be not able to comprehend or express exactly the certain manner how it consists together with Gods Eternall Prescience, and Decrees, which exceed my weak capacity, yet I ought to adhere to that truth, which is manifest. But *T. H.* his opinion of the absoute necessity of all events, by reason of their antecedent determination in their extrinse-

cali

call and neceſſary cauſes, is no ſuch certain Truth, but an innovation, a ſtrange paradox, without probable grounds, rejected by all Authours, yea, by all the world. Neither, is the manner how the ſecond cauſes do operate ſo obſcure, or ſo tranſcendent above the reach of reaſon, as the Eternall Decrees of God are. And therefore in both theſe reſpects he cannot challenge the ſame priviledge. I am in profeſſion of an old truth derived by inheritance or ſucceſſion from mine anceſtors. And therefore, though I were not able to clear every quirk in Law, yet I might juſtly hold my poſſeſſion untill a better title were ſhewed for another. He is no old Poſſeſſor, but a new Pretender, and is bound to make good his claime by evident proofs, not by weak and inconſequent ſuppoſitions, or inducements, ſuch as thoſe are which he uſeth here, of *praiſes, diſpraiſes, rewards, puniſhments, the memory of good and evill ſequells, and events,* which may incline the will, but neither can nor do neceſſitate the will. Nor by uncertain and accidentall inferences ſuch as this, *The memory of praiſes, diſpraiſes, rewards, puniſhments, good and evill ſequells do make us* (he ſhould ſay diſpoſe us) *to elect what we elect, but the memory of theſe things is from the ſenſe, and the ſenſe from the operation of the externall objects, and the Agency of externall objects is onely from God, therefore all actions, even of free and voluntary Agents, are neceſſary.* To paſs by all the other great imperfections, which are to be found in this Sorite. It is juſt like that old Sophiſticall piece: He

O 2

that

that drinks well, sleeps well, he that sleeps well, thinks no hurt, he that thinks no hurt lives well, therefore he that drinks well lives well.

In the very last passage of my discourse, I proposed mine own private opinion, how it might be made appear, that the Eternall Prescience and Decrees of God are consistent with true liberty and contingency. And this I set down, in as plain tearmes as I could, or as so profound a speculation would permit, which is almost wholly misunderstood by *T. H.* and many of my words wrested to a wrong sense. As first, where I speak of the aspect of God, that is his view, his knowledge, by which the most free and contingent actions were manifest to him from eternity, Heb. 4. 11. *All things are naked and open to his eyes*, and this not discursively, but intuitively, not by externall species, but by his internall Essence; He confounds this with the Will, and the Decrees of God: Though he found not the word *Aspect* before in this discourse, he might have found prescience. Secondly, he chargeth me that hitherto I have maintained, that *Liberty and the Decrees of God, are irreconcilable*. If I have said any such thing, my heart never went along with my pen. No, but his reason why he chargeth me on this manner, is because I have maintained, that *Liberty and the absolute necessity of all things are irreconcilable*. That is true indeed. What then? *Why* (saith he) *Necessity and Gods Decrees are all one*. How all one? that were strange indeed,

Necessity

Necessity may be a consequent of Gods Decrees, it cannot be the Decree it self. But to cut his argument short. God hath decreed all effects which come to pass in time, yet not all after the same manner, but according to the distinct natures, capacities and conditions of his creatures, which he doth not destroy by his Decree; Some he acteth, with some he cooperateth by speciall influence, and some he onely permitteth. Yet this is no idle or bare permission, seeing he doth concurre both by way of generall influence, giving power to act, and also by disposing all events necessary, free, and contingent to his own glory. Thirdly, he chargeth me, that *I allow all men to be of his opinion, save onely those that conceive in their minds a* Nunc stans, *or how eternity is an indivisible point, rather than an everlasting succession*. But I have given no such allowance. I know, there are many other wayes proposed by Divines, for reconciling the Eternall Prescience, and Decrees of God, with the Liberty and Contingency of second causes, some of which may please other judgments better than this of mine. Howsoever, though a man could comprehend none of all these wayes, yet remember what I said, that a certain truth ought not to be rejected, because we are not able, in respect of our weakness, to understand the certain manner, or reason of it. I know, the Load-stone hath an attractive power to draw the Iron to it; And yet I know not how it comes to have such a power.

But the chiefest difficulty, which offers it self in this

this Section is, whether Eternity be an indivisible point (as I maintain it) or an everlasting succession, as he would have it. According to his constant use, he gives no answer to what was urged by me, but pleads against it from his own incapacity. *I never could conceive, saith he, how eternity should be an indivisible point.* I believe, that neither we, nor any man els can comprehend it so cleerly, as we do these inferiour things. The neerer that any thing comes to the essence of God, the more remote it is from our apprehension. But shall we therefore make potentialities, and successive duration, and former and later, or a part without a part (as they say) to be in God? Because we are not able to understand cleerly the divine perfection, we must not therefore attribute any imperfection to him.

He saith moreover, that *he understands as little how it can be true which I say, that God is not just but Justice it self, not eternall but Eternity it self.* It seemes howsoever he be versed in this question, that he hath not troubled his head overmuch with reading School-Divines, or Metaphysicians, if he make faculties or qualities to be in God, really distinct from his essence. God is a most simple or pure act, which can admit no composition of substance and accidents. Doth he think that the most perfect Essence of God cannot act sufficiently without faculties and qualities? The infinite perfection of the Divine essence, excludes all passive or receptive powers, and cannot be perfected more than it is by any
acci-

accidents. The attributes of God, are not divers vertues, or qualities in him, as they are in the creatures, but really one and the same, with the Divine Essence, and among themselves. They are attributed to God, to supply the defect of our capacity, who are not able to understand that which is to be known of God, under one name, or one act of the understanding.

Furthermore he saith, that *he understands not how I conclude from hence, that Eternity is an indivisible point, and not a succession.* I will help him. The Divine Substance is indivisible; But Eternity is the Divine Substance. The major is evident, because God is *actus simplicissimus*, a most simple act, wherein there is no manner of composition, neither of matter and forme, nor of subject and accidents, nor of parts, &c. and by consequence no divisibility. The minor hath been cleerly demonstrated in mine answer to his last doubt, and is confessed by all men, that whatsoever is in God, is God.

Lastly he saith. He conceives not *how it can be said, that an infinite point, wherein is no succession, can comprehend all time which is successive.* I answer, that it doth not comprehend it formally as time is successive, but eminently and virtually, as Eternity is infinite. To day all Eternity is coexistent with this day. To morrow all Eternity will be coexistent with to morrow, and so in like manner with all the parts of time, being it self without parts. He saith, *He finds not these phrases in the Scripture.* No, but he may find the thing in the Scripture, that God is
infinite

infinite in all his attributes, and not capable of any imperfection.

And so to shew his antipathy against the School-men, that he hath no liberty or power to contain himself, when he meets with any of of their phrases or tenets, he falls into another paroxisme or fit of inveighing against them; And so concludes his answer with a *plaudite* to himself, because he had defeated both my squadrons of arguments, and reserves of distinctions,

Dicite Io Paan, & Io bis dicite Paan.

But because his eye-sight was weak, and their backs were towards him, he quite mistook the matter. Those whom he see rowted and running away were his own scattered forces.

T. H.

My opinion about Liberty and Necessity.

Numb. 25. *First, I conceive that when it cometh into a mans mind, to do or not to do some certain action, if he have no time to deliberate the doing or abstaining, necessarily followeth the present thought he had of the good or evill consequence thereof to himself. As for example, in suddain anger the action shall follow the thought of of revenge, in suddain fear the thought of escape. Also when a man hath time to deliberate, but deliberates not, because never any thing appeared, that could make him doubt of the consequence, the action followes his opinion of the goodness or harm of it. These actions I call voluntary. He, if I understand him aright, calls them Spontaneous, I call them voluntary, because those actions that follow immediatly the last appetite are voluntary.*

luntary. *And here where there is one onely appetite, that one is the last.*

Besides, I see 'tis reasonable to punish a rash action, which could not be justly done by man, unless the same were voluntary: For no action of a man can be said to be without deliberation, though never so suddain, because 'tis supposed he had time to deliberate all the precedent time of his life, whether he should do that kind of action or not. And hence it is, that he that killeth in a suddain passion of anger, shall neverthelesse be justly put to death, because all the time wherein he was able to consider, whether to kill were good or evill, shall be held for one continuall deliberation, and consequently the killing shall be judged to proceed from election.

J. D.

THis part of *T. H.* his discourse hangs together like a sick mans dreames. Even now he tells us, that *a man may have time to deliberate, yet not deliberate*; By and by he saith, that *no action of a man, though never so suddain, can be said to be without deliberation.* He tells us Numb. 33. that *the scope* of this section is *to shew what is spontaneous.* Howbeit he sheweth onely what is voluntary; so making voluntary and spontaneous to be all one, whereas before he had told us, that *every spontaneous action is not voluntary, because indeliberate. Nor every voluntary action spontaneous, if it proceed from fear.* Now he tells us, that *those actions, which follow the last appetite, are voluntary, and where there is one onely appetite, that is the last.* But before

before he told us, that *voluntary præsupposeth some præcedent deliberation and Meditation of what is likely to follow, both upon the doing and abstaining from the action.* He defines Liberty, Numb. 29. to be *the absence of all extrinsecall impediments to action.* And yet in his whole discourse he laboureth to make good, that whatsoever is not done, is therefore not done, because the Agent was necessitated by extrinsecall causes not to do it. Are not extrinsecall causes, which determine him not to do it, extrinsecall impediments to action. So no man shall be free to do any thing, but that which he doth actually. He defines a free Agent to be *him, who hath not made an end of deliberating*, Numb. 28. And yet defines liberty to be *an absence of outward impediments.* There may be outward impediments, even whilest he is deliberating. As a man deliberates whether he shall play at Tennis, and at the same time the door of the Tennis-court is fast locked against him. And after a man hath ceased to deliberate, there may be no outward impediments, as when a man resolves not to play at Tennis, because he finds himself ill disposed, or because he will not hazard his mony. So the same person, at the same time, should be free and not free, not free and free. And as he is not firme to his own grounds, so he confounds all things, the *mind* and the *will*, the *estimative faculty* and the *understanding*, *imagination* with *deliberation*, the end with the means, humane *will* with the *sensitive appetite*, *rationall hope or fear*, with *irrationall passions*, *inclinations* with *intentions*,

tions, A *beginning of Being* with a *beginning of working*. *Sufficiency* with *efficiency*. So as the greatest difficulty is to find out what he aimes at. So as I had once resolved not to answer this part of his discourse, yet upon better advise, I will take a brief survey of it also; and shew how far I assent unto, or dissent from that which I conceive to be his meaning.

And first, concerning suddain passions, as Anger or the like; That which he saith, that *the action doth necessarily follow the thought*, is thus far true, that those actions, which are altogether undeliberated and do proceed from suddain and violent passions, or *motus primo primis*, which surprise a man, and give him no time to advise with reason, are not properly and actually in themselves free, but rather necessary actions, as when a man runs away from a Cat or a Custard, out of a secret antipathy.

Secondly, as for those actions *wherein actuall deliberation seemes not necessary, because never any thing appeared that could make a man doubt of the consequence*. I do confess, that actions done by vertue of a precedent deliberation, without any actuall deliberation in the present when the act is done, may notwithstanding be truly, both voluntary and free acts, yea, in some cases, and in some sense more free, than if they were actually deliberated of in present. As one who hath acquired by former deliberation and experience, an habit to play upon the Virginall, needs not deliberate what man, or what Jack he much touch, nor what finger of his hand he must move to

play

play such a lesson; Yea, if his mind should be fixed, or intent to every motion of his hand, or every touch of a string, it would hinder his play, and render the action more troublesome to him. Wherefore I believe, that not onely his playing in generall, but every motion of his hand, though it be not presently deliberated of, is a free act, by reason of his precedent deliberation. So then (saving improprieties of speech, as calling that voluntary which is free, and limiting the will to the last appetite, and other mistakes, as that no act can be said to be without deliberation) we agree also for the greater part in this second observation.

Thirdly, whereas he saith, that *some suddain acts, proceeding from violent passions, which surprise a man, are justly punished*, I grant they are so sometimes, but not for his reason, because they have been formerly actually deliberated of, but because they were virtually deliberated of, or because it is our faults, that they were not actually deliberated of, whether it was a fault of pure negation, that is, of not doing our duty onely, or a fault of bad disposition also, by reason of some vitious habit, which we had contracted by our former actions. To do a necessary act is never a fault, nor justly punishable, when the necessity is inevitably imposed upon us by extrinsecall causes. As if a child before he had the use of reason shall kill a man in his passion, yet because he wanted malice to incite him to it, and reason to restrain him from it, he shall not dy for it in the strict rules of particular Justice, unless there be be some mixture of publick Justice in the case. But if the necessity be contracted by our selves, and by our own faults, it is justly punishable. As he who by his wanton thoughts in the day-time, doth procure his own nocturnall pollution. A man cannot deliberate in his sleep, yet it is accounted a sinfull act, and consequently, a free act, that is not actually free in its self, but virtually free in its causes, and though it be not expresly willed and chosen, yet it is tacitely and implicitely willed and chosen, when that is willed and chosen from whence it was necessarily produced. By the Leviticall Law, if a man digged a pit, and left it uncovered, so that his neighbours Oxe, or his Asse, did fall into it, he was bound to make reparation, not because he did chose to leave it uncovered on purpose that such a mischance might happen, but because he did freely omit, that which he ought to have done, from whence this dammage proceeded to his neighbour. Lastly, there is great difference between the first motions, which sometimes are not in our power, and subsequent acts of killing or stealing, or the like, which alwaies are in our power, if we have the use of reason, or els it is our own fault, that they are not in our power. Yet to such hasty acts done in hot blood, the Law is not so severe, as to those which are done upon long deliberation, and prepensed malice, unless (as I said) there be some mixture of publick Justice in it. He that steales an horse deliberately may be more punishable by the Law, than he that kills the owner by Chance-medley. Yet the death of

the

the owner was more noxious (to use his phrase) and more dammageable to the family, than the stealth of the horse. So far was *T. H.* mistaken in that also, that the right to kill men, doth proceed meerly from their being noxious, *Numb.* 14.

T. H.

Numb. 26. *Secondly, I conceive when a man deliberates, whether he shall do a thing or not do a thing, that he does nothing els but consider, whether it be better for himself to do it, or not to do it. And to consider an action, is to imagine the consequences of it, both good and evill, from whence is to be inferred, that deliberation is nothing but alternate imagination, of the good and evill sequells of an action or (which is the same thing) alternate hope and fear, or alternate appetite to do, or quit the action of which he deliberateth.*

J. D.

IF I did not know what deliberation was, I should be little believed in my knowledge by this description. Sometimes he makes it to be a consideration, or an act of the understanding, sometimes an imagination, or an act of the fancy, sometimes he makes it to be an alternation of passions, hope and fear. Sometimes he makes it concerne the end, sometimes to concerne the means. So he makes it I know not what. The truth is this in brief. *Deliberation is an inquiry made by reason, whether this or that definitely considered, be a good and fit means, or indefinitely what are good and fit means to be chosen for attaining some wished end.*

T. H.

T. H.

Thirdly, I conceive, that in all deliberations, Numb. 27. that is to say, in all alternate succession of contrary appetites, the last is, that which we call the Will, and is immediatly before the doing of the action, or next before the doing of it become impossible. All other appetites to do and to quit, that come upon a man during his deliberation, are usually called intentions, and inclinations, but not wills, there being but one will, which also in this case may be called last will, though the intention change often.

J. D.

Still here is nothing but confusion, he confounds the faculty of the will, with the act of volition, he makes the will to be the last part of deliberation. He makes the intention, which is a most proper and elicite act of the will, *or a willing of the end, as it is to be attained by certain means*, to be no willing at all, but onely some antecedaneous *inclination* or propension. He might as well say, that the uncertain agitation of the needle hither and thither, to find out the Pole, and the resting or fixing of it self directly towards the Pole, were both the same thing. But the grossest mistake is, that he will acknowledge no act of a mans will, to be his will, But onely the last act, which he calls the last will. If the first were no will, how comes this to be the last will? According to this doctrine, the will of a man should be as unchangeable as the Will of God, at least so long as there is a possibility to effect it. According to this doctrine

concu-

concupiscence with consent should be no sin, for that which is not truly willed is not a sin; Or rather should not be at all, unless either the act followed, or were rendred impossible by some intervening circumstances. According to this doctrine no man can say, this is my will, because he knowes not yet, whether it shall be his last appeal. The truth is, there be many acts of the will, both in respect of the means, and of the end. But that act, which makes a mans actions to be truly free, is Election, which is the *deliberate chosing or refusing, of this or that means, or the acceptation of one means before another, where divers are represented by the understanding.*

T. H.

Numb. 28. *Fourthly, that those actions, which man is said to do upon deliberation, are said to be voluntary, and done upon choise and election. So that voluntary action, and action proceeding from election, is the same thing. And that of a voluntary Agent, 'tis all one to say he is free, and to say, he hath not made an end of deliberating.*

J. D.

This short Section might pass without an animadversion but for two things. The one is, that he confounds a voluntary act with a free act. A free act is onely that which proceeds from the free election of the rationall will after deliberation, but every act that proceeds from the sensitive appetite of man or beast, without deliberation or election, is truly voluntary. The other thing observable is his conclusion, that *it is all one to say a man is free, and to say, he hath* not

not made an end of deliberating. Which confession of his, overturnes his whole structure of absolute necessity, for if every Agent be necessitated to act what he doth act by a necessary and naturall flux of extrinsecall causes, then he is no more free before he deliberates, or whilest he deliberates, than he is after, but by *T. H.* his confession here, he is more free, whilest he deliberates, than he is after; And so after all his flourishes, for an absolute or extrinsecall necessity, he is glad to sit himself down, and rest contented with an hypotheticall necessity, which no man ever denied or doubted of. Ascribing the necessitation of a man in free acts to his own deliberation, and in indeliberate acts to his last thought, *Numb.* 25. what is this to a naturall and speciall influence of extrinsecall causes. Again, *Liberty* (saith he) is *an absence of extrinsecall impediments*, but deliberation doth produce no new extrinsecall impediments, therefore (let him chose which part he will) either he is free after deliberation, by his own doctrine, or he was not free before. Our own deliberation, and the direction of our own understanding, and the election of our own will, do produce an hypotheticall necessity, that the event be such as the understanding hath directed, and the will elected. But forasmuch as the understanding might have directed otherwise, and the will have elected otherwise, this is far from an absolute necessity. Neither doth liberty respect onely future acts, but present acts also. Otherwise God did not freely create the world. In the same instant wherein in the will elects it is free, according to a priority of Nature, though not of time, to elect otherwise. And so in a divided sense, the will is free, even whilest it acts, though in a compounded sense it be not free. Certainly, deliberation doth constitute, not destroy liberty.

T. H.

Numb. 29.

Ifily, I conceive liberty to be rightly defined in this manner. Liberty is the absence of all the impediments to action, that are not contained in the nature, and in the intrinsecall quality of the Agent. As for example, the water is said to descend freely, or to have liberty to descend by the Chanell of the River, because there is no impediment that way, but not across, because the banks are impediments. And though water cannot ascend, yet men never say it wants the liberty to ascend, but the faculty or power, because the impediment is in the nature of the water and intrinsecall. So also we say, he that is tied wants the liberty to go, because the impediment is not in him, but in his bands, whereas we say not so of him that is sick or lame, because the impediment is in himself.

J. D.

How that should be a right definition of liberty which comprehends neither the Genus nor the difference, neither the matter nor the forme of liberty, which doth not so much as accidentally describe liberty by its marks and tokens; How a reall faculty or the Elective power should be defined by a negation, or by an ababsence, is past my understanding, and contrary
to

to all the rules of right Reason, which I have lea[r]ed. Negatives cannot explicate the nature of things defined. By this definition, a stone hath liberty to ascend into the aire, because there is no outward impediment to hinder it, and so a violent act may be a free act. Just like his definition are his instances of the liberty of the water to descend down the Channell, and a sick or a lame mans liberty to goe. The later is an impotence and not a power or a liberty. The former is so far from being a free act, that it is scarce a naturall act, Certainly, the proper naturall motion of water, as of all heavy bodies, is to descend directly downwards towards the center, as we see in rain, which falls down perpendicularly. Though this be far from a free act, which proceeds from a rationall appetite, yet it is a naturall act, and proceeds from a naturall appetite, and hath its reason within in self. So hath not the current of the River in its channell, which must not be ascribed to the proper nature of the water, but either to the generall order of the universe, for the better being and preservation of the creatures (otherwise the waters should not moove in Seas and Rivers as they do, but cover the face of the earth, and possess their proper place between the aire and the earth, according to the degree of their gravity.) Or to an extrinsecall principle, whilest one particle of water thrusteth and forceth forward another, and so comes a current, or at least so comes the current to be more impetuous, to which motion the position of the earth doth contribute

tribute much, both by restraining that fluid body with its banks from disperſing it ſelf, and alſo, by affording way for a faire and eaſy deſcent by its proclivity. He tells us ſadly that *the water wants liberty to go over the banks, becauſe there is an extrinſecall impediment, But to aſcend up the channell it wants not liberty, but power.* Why? Liberty is a power, if it want power to aſcend, it wants liberty to aſcend. But he makes the reaſon why the water aſcends not up the channell, to be intrinſecall, and the reaſon why it aſcends not over the banks to be extrinſecall, as if there were not a riſing of the ground up the channell, as well as up the banks, though it be not ſo diſcernible, nor alwayes ſo ſudden. The naturall appetite of the water is as much againſt the aſcending over the banks, as the aſcending up the channell. And the extrinſecall impediment is as great in aſcending up the channell as over the banks, or rather greater, becauſe there it muſt moove, not onely againſt the riſing ſoile, but alſo againſt the ſucceeding waters, which preſs forward the former. Either the River wants liberty for both, or els it wans liberty for neither.

But to leave his metaphoricall faculties, and his Catachreſticall Liberty. How far is his diſcourſe wide from the true morall liberty, which is in queſtion between us. His former deſcription of a free Agent, that is, *he who hath not made an end of deliberating*, though it was wide from the mark, yet it came much neerer the truth than this definition of Liberty, unleſs perhaps he think that the water hath done deliberating,
whe-

whether it will go over the banks, but hath not done deliberating, whether it will go up the channell.

T. H.

Sixtly, I conceive, nothing taketh beginning Numb. 30 *from it self, but from the action of some other immediate Agent without it self. And that therefore when first a man had an appetite or will, to something, to which immediately before he had no appetite nor will, the cause of his will is not the will it self, but something els, not in his own disposing. So that whereas it is out of controversy that of voluntary actions the will is a necessary cause; And by this which is said the will is also caused by other things whereof it disposeth not, it followeth that voluntary actions have all of them necessary causes, and therefore are necessitated.*

J. D.

This sixt point doth not consist in explicating of tearmes, as the former, but in two proofs, that voluntary actions are necessitated. The former proof stands thus, *Nothing takes beginning from it self, but from some Agent without it self, which is not in its own disposing, therefore &c. concedo omnia,* I grant all he saith, The will doth not take beginning from it self. Whether he understand by *will* the faculty of the will, which is a power of the reasonable soul, it takes not beginning from it self, but from God, who created and infused the Soul into man, and endowed it with this power: Or whether he understand by *will*, the act of willing, it takes not beginning from it self, but from the

faculty

faculty, or from the power of willing, which is in the Soul. This is certain, finite and participated things cannot be from themselves, nor be produced by themselves. What would he conclude from hence? that therefore the act of willing takes not its beginning from the faculty of the will? Or that the faculty is alwayes determined antecedently, extrinsecally to will that which it doth will? He may as soon draw water out of a pumice, as draw any such conclusion out of these premisses. Secondly, for his *taking a beginning*, Either he understands *a beginning of being*, or a *beginning of working and acting*, If he understand a beginning of being, he saith most truly, that nothing hath a beginning of being in time from it self, But this is nothing to his purpose. The question is not between us whether the Soul of man, or the will of man be eternall, But if he understand *a beginning of working or mooving actually*, it is a gross errour. All men know that when a stone descends, or fire ascends, or when water, that hath been heated returnes, to its former temper, the beginning or reason is intrinsecall, and one and the same thing doth moove and is mooved in a diverse respect. It mooves in respect of the form, and it is mooved in respect of the matter. Much more man, who hath a perfect knowledge and prenotion of the end, is most properly said to moove himself. Yet I do not deny but that there are other beginnings of humane actions, which do concur with the will, some outward as the first cause by generall influence, which is evermore requisite, Angells or men by perswading, evill spirits by tempting, the object or end by its appetibility, the understanding by directing. So passions and acquired habits. But I deny that any of these do necessitate or can necessitate the will of man by determining it Physically to one, except God alone, who doth it rarely in extraordinary cases. And where there is no antecedent determination to one, there is no absolute necessity but true Liberty.

His second argument is *ex concessis*, *It is out of controversy* (saith he) *that of voluntary actions the will is a necessary cause*. The argument may be thus reduced. Necessary causes produce necessary effects, but the Will is a necessarie cause of voluntary actions. I might deny his major; Necessary causes do not alwayes produce necessary effects, except they be also necessarily produced, as I have shewed before the burning of *Protagoras* his book. But I answer cleerly to the minor, that the will is not a necessary cause of what it wills in particular actions. It is without *controversy* indeed, for it is without all probability. That it wills, when it wills, is necessary, but that it wills this or that, now or then, is free. More expresly the act of the will may be considered three wayes; Either in respect of its nature, or in respect of its exercise, or in respect of its object. First, for the nature of the act; That which the will wills is necessarily voluntary, because the will cannot be compelled. And in this sense, *it is out of controversy, that the will is a necessary cause of voluntary actions,*

ctions. Secondly, for the exercise of its acts, that is not necessary. The will may either will or suspend its act. Thirdly, for the object that is not necessary but free, the will is not extrinsecally determined to its objects. As for example, The Cardinalls meet in the conclave to chose a Pope, whom they chose he is necessarily Pope. But it is not necessary that they shall chose this or that day. Before they were assembled they might defer their assembling, when they are assembled, they may suspend their election for a day or a week. Lastly, for the person whom they will choose, it is freely in their own power, otherwise if the election were not free, it were void, and no election at all. So that which takes its beginning from the will, is necessarily voluntary, but it is not necessary that the will shall will this or that in particular, as it was necessary, that the person freely elected should be Pope, but it was not necessary, either that the election should be at this time, or that this man should be elected. And therefore voluntary acts in particular, have not necessary causes, that is, they are not necessitated.

T. H.

Numb. 31. *Seventhly, I hold that to be a sufficient cause to which nothing is wanting that is needfull to the producing of the effect. The same is also a necessary cause, for if it be possible, that a sufficient cause shall not bring forth the effect, then there wanted somewhat which was needfull to the producing of it, and so the cause was not sufficient. But if it be impossible that a sufficient cause should*

not

not produce the effect, then is a sufficient cause a necessary cause, (for that is said to produce an effect necessarily, that cannot but produce it) Hence it is manifest, that whatsoever is produced, is produced necessarily, for whatsoever is produced hath had a sufficient cause to produce it, or els it had not been. And therefore also voluntary actions are necessitated.

J. D.

THis section containes a third Argument to proove that all effects are necessary, for clearing whereof it is needfull to consider how a cause may be said to be sufficient or insufficient.

First, severall causes singly considered may be insufficient, and the same taken conjointly be sufficient to produce an effect. As two horses jointly are sufficient to draw a Coach, which either of them singly is insufficient to do. Now to make the effect, that is the drawing of the Coach necessary, it is not onely required, that the two horses be sufficient to draw it, but also that their conjunction be necessary, and their habitude such as they may draw it. If the owner of one of these horses will not suffer him to draw, If the Smith have shod the other in the quick, and lamed him; If the horse have cast a shoe, or be a resty jade, and will not draw but when he list, then the effect is not necessarily produced, but contingently more or less, as the concurrence of the causes is more or less contingent. 1

Secondly, a cause may be said to be sufficient, either because it produceth that effect which is intended; as in the generation of a man, or els, 2

becausе

because it is sufficient to produce that which is produced, as in the generation of a Monster. The former is properly called a sufficient cause, the later a weak and insufficient cause. Now, if the debility of the cause be not necessary, but contingent, then the effect is not necessary, but contingent. It is a rule in Logick, that the conclusion alwayes followes the weaker part. If the premises be but probable, the conclusion cannot be demonstrative. It holds as well in causes as in propositions. No effect can exceed the vertue of its cause. If the ability or debility, of the causes be contingent, the effect cannot be necessary.

3.   Thirdly, that which concernes this question of Liberty from necessity most neerely is. That a cause is said to be sufficient in respect of the ability of it to act, not in respect of its will to act. The concurrence of the will is needfull to the production of a free effect. But the cause may be sufficient, though the will do not concur. As God is sufficient to produce a thousand worlds, but it doth not follow from thence, either that he hath produced them, or that he will produce them. The blood of Christ is a sufficient ransome for all mankind, but it doth not follow therefore, that all mankind shall be actually saved by vertue of his Blood. A man may be a sufficient Tutour, though he will not teach every Scholler, and a sufficient Physitian, though he will not administer to every patient. Forasmuch therefore as the concurrence of the will is needfull to the production of every free effect,

and

and yet the cause may be sufficient, *in sensu diviso*, although the will do not concur. It followes evidently, that the cause may be sufficient, and yet something, which is needfull to the production of the effect, may be wanting, and that every sufficient cause is not a necessary cause.

Lastly, if any man be disposed to wrangle against so clear light, and say, that though the free Agent be sufficient *in sensu diviso*, yet, he is not sufficient, *in sensu composito*, to produce the effect without the concurrence of the will, he saith true, but first, he bewrayes the weakness and the fallacy of the former argument, which is a meer trifling between sufficiency in a divided sense, and sufficiency in a compounded sense. And seeing the concurrence of the will is not predetermined, there is no antecedent necessity before it do concur, and when it hath concurred, the necessity is but hypotheticall, which may consist with liberty.

T. H.

Lastly, I hold that ordinary definition of a free Agent, namely that a free Agent is, that, which when all things are present, which are needfull to produce the effect, can nevertheless not produce it, Implies a contradiction, and is nonsense, being as much as to say, the cause may be sufficient, *that is* necessary, *and yet the effect not follow.*

D. J.

J. D.

THis last point is but a Corollary, or an Inference from the former doctrine, that *every sufficient cause produceth its effect necessarily*, which pillar being taken away the superstructure must needs fall to the ground, having nothing left to support it. *Lastly, I hold* (saith he) *what he is able to proove is something*. So much reason, so much trust, but what he *holds* concernes himself not others. But what holds he? *I hold* (saith he) *that the ordinary definition of a free Agent implies a contradiction, and is non-sense.* That which he calls the *ordinary definition* of liberty is the very definition which is given by the much greater part of Philosophers & Schoolmen. And doth he think that all these spake non-sense? or had no more judgment than to contradict themselves in a definition? He might much better suspect himself, than censure so many. Let us see the definition it self: *A free Agent is that, which when all things are present, that are needfull to produce the effect, can neverthelesse not produce it.* I acknowledge the old definition of Liberty, with little variation. But I cannot see this *non-sense*, nor discover this *contradiction*. For in these words *all things needfull*, or *all things requisite*, the actuall determination of the will is not included. But by *all things needfull or requisite.* All necessary power either operative or elective, all necessarie instruments and adjuments extrinsecall and intrinsecall, and all conditions are intended. As he that hath pen and ink, and paper, a table, a

desk

desk, and leisure, the art of writing, and the free use of his hand, hath all things requisite to write if he will, and yet he may forbear, if he will. Or as he that hath men and mony, and armes, and munition, and shipps, and a just cause, hath all things requisite for war, yet he may make peace, if he will. Or as the King proclaimed in the Gospell, Matth. 22. 4. *I have prepared my dinner, my oxen and my fatlings are killed, all things are ready, come unto the marriage.* According to *T. H.* his doctrine, the guests might have told him, that he said not truly, for their own wills were not ready. And indeed if the will were (as he conceives it is) necessitated extrinsecally to every act of willing, if it had no power to forbear willing what it doth will, nor to will what it doth not will, then if the will were wanting, something requisite to the producing of the effect was wanting. But now when Science and conscience, reason and Religion, our own and other mens experience doth teach us, that the will hath a dominion over its own acts to will, or nill without extrinsecall necessitation. If the power to will be present *in actu primo*, determinable by our selves, then there is no necessary power wanting in this respect to the producing of the effect.

Secondly, these words *to act or not to act, to work or not to work, to produce or not to produce,* have reference to the effect. not as a thing which is already done, or doing, but as a thing to be done. They imply not the actuall production but the producibility of the effect. But when once

once the will hath actually concurred with, all other causes and conditions, and circumstances, then the effect is no more possible, or producible, but it is in being, and actually produced. Thus he takes away the subject-of the question. The question is whether effects producible be free from necessity. He shuffles out *effects producible*, and thrusts in their places *effects produced*, or which are in the act of *production*. Wherefore I conclude, that it is neither *non-sense* nor *contradiction* to say, that a free Agent, when all things requisite to produce the effect are present, may nevertheless not produce it.

T. H.

Numb. 33. *For my first five points where it is explicated, First, what Spontaneity is, Secondly, what Deliberation is, Thirdly, what Will, Propension and Appetite is, Fourthly, what a free Agent is, Fiftly, what Liberty is, There can be no other proof offered, but every mans own experience, by reflecting on himself, and remembring what he useth to have in his mind, that is what he himself meaneth, when he saith, an action is spontaneous, A man deliberates, such is his will, That Agent, or that action is free. Now, he that so reflecteth on himself cannot but be satisfied, but that deliberation is the considering of the good & evill sequells of the action to come, That by Spontaneity, is meant inconsiderate proceeding, (for els nothing is meant by it.) That will is the last act of our Deliberation. That a free Agent, is he that can do, if he will, and forbear, if he will. And that Liberty*
berty

berty *is the absence of externall impediments: But to those that out of custome speak not what they conceive, but what they hear, and are not able, or will not take the pains to consider what they think, when they hear such words, no argument can be sufficient, because experience, and matter of fact is not verified by other mens Arguments, but by every mans own sense, and memory. For example, how can it be prooved, that to love a thing, and to think it good are all one, to a man that does not mark his own meaning by those words. Or how can it be prooved that Eternity is not* nunc Stans, *to a man that sayes these words by custome, and never considers how he can conceive the thing it self in his mind. Also the sixt point, that a man cannot imagine any thing to begin without a cause, can no other way be made known but by trying how he can imagine it. But if he try, he shall find as much reason (if there be no cause of the thing) to conceive, it should begin at one time as another, that is, he hath equall reason to think, it should begin at all times, which is impossible. And therefore he must think there was some speciall cause, why it began then rather than sooner or later, or els, that it began never, but was Eternall.*

J. D.

Now at length he comes to his main proofs; He that hath so confidently censured the whole current of School-men and Philosophers of *non-sense*, had need to produce strong evidence for himself. So he calls his reasons, Numb. 36. *demonstrative proofs*. All demonstrations are either from the cause or the effect, not from private

private notions and conceptions, which we have in our minds. That which he calls a demonstration deserves not the name of an intimation. He argues thus; *That which a man conceives in his mind, by these words Spontaneity, Deliberation, &c. that they are.* This is his proposition which I deny. The true natures of things are not to be judged by the private *ideas*, or conceptions of men, but by their causes and formall reasons. Ask an ordinary person what *upwards* signifies, and whether our Antipodes have their heads upwards or downwards; And he will not stick to tell you, that if his head be upwards, theirs must needs be downwards. And this is because he knowes not the formall reason thereof. That the Heavens incircle the earth, and what is towards heaven is upwards. This same erronious notion of *vpwards* and *downwards* before the true reason was fully discovered, abused more than ordinary capacities, as appeares by their arguments of *penduli homines*, and *pendulæ arbores*. Again, what do men conceive ordinary by this word *empty*, as when they say an empty vessell, or by this word *Body*, as when they say, there is no body in that roome, they intend not to exclude the aire, either out of the vessell, or out of the roome. Yet reason tells us, that the vessell is not truly empty, and that the aire is a true body. I might give an hundred such like instances. He, who leaves the conduct of his understanding to follow vulgar notions, shall plunge himself into a thousand errours, like him who leaves a certaine guide to follow an *ignis fatuus*, or a Will, with the wispe.

So

So his propofition is falfe. His reafon, *That matter of fact is not verified by other mens Arguments, but by every mans own fenfe and memory*, is likewife maimed on both fides, whether we hear fuch words, or not, is matter of fact, and fenfe is the proper judge of it. But what thefe words do, or ought truely to fignifie is not to be judged by fenfe but by reafon. Secondly, reafon may, and doth oftentimes correct fenfe, even about its proper object. Senfe tells us that the Sun is no bigger than a good Ball, but reafon demonftrates, that it is many times greater than the whole Globe of the earth. As to his inftance, *How can it be proved, that to love a thing, and to think it good, is all one to a man that doth not make his own meaning by thefe words*, I confefs, it cannot be proved, for it is not true. Beauty and likenefs, and love, do conciliate love as much as goodnefs, *cos amoris amor*. Love is a paffion of the will, but to judge of goodnefs is an act of the underftanding. A Father may love an ungracious Childe, and yet not efteem him good. A man loves his own houfe better than another mans, yet he cannot but efteem many others better than his own. His other inftance, *How can it be proved that eternity is not* nunc ftans, *to a man that fayes thefe words by cuftom, and never confiders how he can conceive the thing it felf in his minde*, is juft like the former, not to be proved by reafon, but by fancie, which is the way he takes. And it is not unlike the counfel, which one gave to a *Novice* about the choife of his wife to advice with the Bels, as he fancied fo they founded, either take her, or leave her.

    Then for his affumption it is as defective as his

Q   propo-

proposition, That *by these words spontaneity*, &c. *men do understand as he conceives*. No rational man doth conceive a *spontaneous* action, and an *indeliberate* action to be all one, every *indeliberate* action is not *spontaneous*. The fire considers not whether it should burn, yet the burning of it is not *spontaneous*. Neither is every *spontaneous* action indeliberate, a man may deliberate what he will eat, and yet eat it *spontaneously*. Neither doth *deliberation* properly signifie the *considering of the good and evil sequels of an action to come*: But the considering whether this be a good and fit means, or the best, and fittest means for obtaining such an end. The Physician doth not deliberate whether he should cure his Patient, but by what means he should cure him. Deliberation is of the means not of the end. Much less doth any man conceive with *T. H.* that deliberation is an *imagination*, or an act of fancy, not of reason, common to men of discretion with mad men, and natural fools and children, and bruit beasts. Thirdly, neither doth any understanding man conceive, or can conceive, either that the *will is an act of our deliberation*, the understanding and the will are two distinct faculties, or that *onely the last appetite is to be called our will*. So no man should be able to say this is my will, because he knows not whether he shall persevere in it, or not. Concerning the fourth point we agree that *he is a free Agent that can do, if he will, and forbear if he will*. But I wonder how this dropped from his pen, what is now become of his absolute necessity of all things? If a man be free to do and to forbear any thing, will he make himself guilty of the *non-sence* of the School-men; and run with them

them into contradictions for company? It may be he will say he can do if he will, and forbear if he will, but he cannot will if he will. This will not serve his turn, for if the cause of a free action, that is, the will to be determined, then the effect, or the action it self is likewise determined, a determined cause cannot produce an undetermined effect, either the Agent can will, and forbear to will, or else he cannot do, and forbear to do. But we differ wholy about the fifth point. He who conceives *liberty* aright, conceives both a *liberty in the subject* to will, or not to will, and a *liberty to the object* to will this, or that, and a *liberty from impediments*. T. H. by a new way of his own cuts off the *liberty of the subject*, as if a stone was free to ascend, or descend, because it hath no outward impediment. And the *liberty towards the object*, as if the Needle touched with the Load-stone were free to point, either towards the North, or towards the South, because there is not a Barrecado in its way to hinder it, yea, he cuts off the *liberty from inward impediments* also: As if an Hawk were at liberty to fly when her wings are plucked, but not when they are tied. And so he makes *liberty from extrinsecal impediments* to be compleat liberty, so he ascribes *liberty* to bruit beasts, and *liberty* to Rivers, and by consequence makes Beasts and Rivers to be capeable of sin and punishment. Assuredly, *Xerxes*, who caused the Hellespont to be beaten with so many stripes, was of this opinion. Lastly, T. H. his reason, that *it is custom, or want of ability, or negligence which makes a man conceive otherwise*, is but a begging of that which he should prove. Other men consider as seriously as himself, with as much judgement as himself, with less prejudice than himself, and yet they can apprehend no such sense of these words, would he have other men feign that they see fiery Dragons in the Air, because he affirms confidently that he sees them, and wonders why others are so blinde as not to see them?

The reason for the sixth point is like the former, a phantastical, or imaginative reason. *How can a man imagine any thing to begin without a cause, or if it should begin without a cause, why it should begin at this time rather than at that time?* He saith truely, nothing can *begin* without a cause, that is *to be*, but it may *begin to act* of it self without any other cause. Nothing can begin without a cause, but many things may begin, and do begin without necessary causes. A free cause may as wel choose his time when he will begin, as a necessary cause be determined extrinsically when it must begin. And although free effects cannot be foretold, because they are not certainly predetermined in their causes, yet when the free causes do determine themselves, they are of as great certainty as the other. As when I see a Bell ringing, I can conceive the cause of it as well why it rings now, as I know the interposition of the earth to be the cause of the Eclipse of the Moon. Or the most certain occurrent in the nature of things.

And now that I have answered *T. H.* his Arguments drawn from the private conceptions of men concerning the sense of words, I desire him seriously without prejudice to examine himself and those natural notions, which he findes in himself, not of words, but of things, these are from nature, those are

are by imposition, whether he doth not finde by experience that he doth many things, which he might have left undone if he would, and omits many things which he might have done if he would, whether he doth not somethings out of meer animosity, and will without either regard to the direction of right reason, or serious respect of what is honest, or profitable; onely to shew that he will have a dominion over his own actions, as we see ordinarily in Children, and wise men finde at some times in themselves by experience. And I apprehend this very defence of necessity against liberty to be partly of that kinde. Whether he is not angry with those who draw him from his study, or cross him in his desires, if they be necessitated to do it, why should he be angry with them, any more than he is angry with a sharp winter, or a rainy day that keeps him at home against his antecedent will, whether he doth not sometime blame himself, and say, *O what a fool was I to do thus and thus*, or wish to himself, *O that I had been wise*, or, *O that I had not done such an act.* If he have no dominion over his actions, if he be irresistibly necessitated to all things what he doth, he might as well wish, *O that I had not breathed*, or blame himself for growing old, *O what a fool was I to grow old.*

T. H.

For the seventh point, that all events have necessary causes, it is there proved in that they have sufficient causes. Further, Let us in this place also suppose any event never so casuall, as for example, the throwing Ambs-ace upon a paire of Dice, and see if it must not have been ne- Numb. 34.

cessary before it was thrown, for, seeing it was thrown, it had a beginning, and consequently a sufficient cause to produce it, consisting partly in the Dice, partly in the outward things, as the posture of the parties hand, the measure of force applied by the caster, The posture of the parts of the Table, and the like; In summe, there was nothing wanting that was necessarily requisite to the producing of that particular cast, and consequently, that cast was necessarily thrown. For if it had not been thrown, there had wanted somewhat requisite to the throwing of it, and so the cause had not been sufficient. In the like manner it may be proved that every other accident, how contingent soever it seeme, or how voluntary soever it be, is produced necessarily, which is that J. D. *disputes against. The same also may be proved in this manner, Let the case be put, for example of the weather,* Tis necessary that to morrow it shall rain, or not rain. *If therefore it be not necessary, it shall rain, it is necessary it shall not rain. Otherwise it is not necessary that the proposition.* It shall rain, or it shall not rain, *should be true. I know there are some that say, it may necessarily be true, that one of the two shall come to pass, but not singly that it shall rain, or it shall not rain. Which is as much as to say, One of them is necessary, yet neither of them is necessary; And therefore to seeme to avoid, that absurdity they make a distinction, that neither of them is true* determinatè *but* indeterminate; *Which distinction, either signifies no more than this,* One of them is true, but we know not which,
and

and so the necessity remains, though we know it not: Or if the meaning of the distinction be not that, it has no meaning. And they might as well have said, One of them is true, Tytyrice but neither of them Tupatulice.

J. D.

His former proof, that all sufficient causes are necessary causes is answered before, *Numb.* 31. And his two instances of casting Ambs-ace, & raining to morrow, are altogether impertinent to the question now agitated between us, for two reasons. First, our present controversie is concerning free actions, which proceed from the liberty of mans will, both his instances are of contingent actions, which proceed from the indetermination, or contingent concurrence of natural causes. First, that there are free actions, which proceed meerly from election, without any outward necessitation is a truth so evident, as that there is a Sun in the Heavens, and he that doubteth of it may as well doubt whether there be a shell without the Nut, or a stone within the Olive. A man proportions his time each day, and allots so much to his Devotions, so much to his Study, so much to his Diet, so much to his Recreations, so much to necessary, or civil visits, so much to his rest, he who will seek for I know not what causes of all this without himself, except that good God who hath given him a reasonable Soul, may as well seek for a cause of the Egyptian *Pyramides* among the Crocodiles of *Nilus*. Secondly, for mixt actions which proceed from the concurrence of free and natural Agents, though they be not free, yet they are not necessary, as to keep my former instance, a man walking through a street of a Citie to do his occasions, a Tile falls from an House and breaks his head, the breaking of his head was not necessary, for he did freely choose to go that way without any necessitation, neither was it free, for he did not deliberate of that accident, therefore it was contingent, and by undoubted consequence there are contingent actions in the World which are not free. Most certainly by the concurrence of free causes, as God, the good and bad Angels and men, with natural Agents sometimes on purpose, and sometimes by accident many events happen, which otherwise had never hapned; many effects are produced which otherwise had never been produced. And admitting such things to be contingent not necessary, all their consequent effects, not onely immediate, but mediate must likewise be contingent, that is to say, such as do not proceed from a continued connexion and succession of necessary causes, which is directly contrary to *T. H.* his opinion.

Thirdly, for the actions of bruit beasts, though they be not free, though they have not the use of reason to restrain their appetites from that which is sensitively good by the consideration of what is rationaly good, or what is honest, and though their fancies be determined by nature to some kindes of work, yet to think that every individual action of theirs, and each animal motion of theirs, even to the least murmure, or gesture is bound by the chain of unalterable necessity to the extrinsecal causes or objects, I see no ground for it. Christ saith *one of these Sparrows doth not fall to the ground without your Heavenly Father*, that is without an influence of power from him, or exempted fro his disposition,
he

he doth not say which your heavenly Father casteth not down. Lastly, for the natural actions of inanimate Creatures, wherein there is not the least concurrence of any free, or voluntary Agents, the questiõ is yet more doubtfull, for many things are called cõtingent in respect of us, because we know not the cause of them, which really & in themselves are not contingent, but necessary. Also many things are contingent in respect of one single cause, either actually hindred, or in possibility to be hindred, which are necessary in respect of the joynt concurrence of all collateral causes. But whether there be a necessary connexion of all natural causes from the beginning, so as they must all have concurred as they have done, & in the same degree of power, & have been deficient as they have beẽ in all events whatsoever, would require a further examination if it were pertinent to this question of liberty; but it is not. It is sufficient to my purpose to have shewed that all elective actions are free from absolute necessity. And moreover, that the concurrence of voluntary and free Agents with natural causes, both upon purpose and accidentally hath helped them to produce many effects, which otherwise they had not produced, and hindred them from producing many effects, which otherwise they had produced. And that if this in intervention of voluntary and free Agents had been more frequent than it hath been, (as without doubt it might have been) many natural events had been otherwise than they are. And therefore he might have spared his instances of casting *Ambs-ace* and raining to morrow. And first for his casting *Ambs-ace*. If it be thrown by a fair Gamester with indifferent Dice, it is a mixt action, the casting of the

Dice

Dice is free, but the casting of *Ambs-ace* is contingent, a man may deliberate whether he will cast the Dice, or not, but it were folly to deliberate whether he will cast *Ambs-ace*, or not, because it is not in his power, unless he be a cheater that can cogge the Dice, or the Dice be false Dice, & then the contingency, or the degree of contingency ceaseth, accordingly as the Caster hath more, or less cunning, or as the figure, or making of the Dice doth incline them to *Ambs-ace* more than to another cast, or necessitate them to this cast and no other. Howsoever so far as the cast is free, or contingent, so far it is not necessary. And where necessity begins, there liberty and contingency do cease to be: Likewise his other instance of raining, or not raining, to morrow is not of a free elective act, nor alwayes of a contingent act. In some Countries as they have their *stati venti* their certain winds at set seasons, so they have their certain and set rains. The *Æthiopian* rains are supposed to be the cause of the certain inundation of *Nilus*. In some eastern Countries they have rain onely twice a year, and those constant, which the Scriptures call *the former and the later rain*. In such places not onely the causes do act determinately and necessarily, but also the determination, or necessity of the event is foreknown to the inhabitants. In our Climate the natural causes cœlestial and sublunary do not produce rain so necessarily at set times, neither can we say so certainly and infallibly, it will rain to morrow, or it will not rain to morrow. Neverthelesse, it may so happen that the causes are so disposed and determined, even in our climate, that this proposition, it will rain to morrow, or it will not rain, to morrow,

morrow may be neceſſary in it ſelf, and the Prognoſticks, or tokens may be ſuch in the sky, in our own bodies, in the creatures, animate and inanimate as weather-glaſſes, &c. that it may become probably true to us that it will rain to morrow, or it will not rain to morrow. But ordinarily it is a contingent propoſition to us, whether it be contingent alſo in it ſelf, that is, whether the concurrence of the cauſes were abſolutely neceſſary, whether the vapours, or matter of the rain may not yet be diſperſed, or otherwiſe conſumed, or driven beyond our coaſt, is a ſpeculation which no way concerns this queſtion. So we ſee one reaſon why his two inſtances are altogether impertinent, becauſe they are of actions which are not free, nor elective, nor ſuch as proceed from the liberty of mans will.

Secondly, our diſpute is about abſolute neceſſity, his proofs extend onely to Hypothetical neceſſity. Our queſtion is, whether the concurrence and determination of the cauſes were neceſſary before they did concur, or were determined. He proves that the effect is neceſſary after the cauſes have concurred, and are determined. The freeſt actions of God, or man, are neceſſary by ſuch a neceſſity of ſuppoſition. And the moſt contingent events that are, as I have ſhewed plainly, *Numb.* 3. where his inſtance of *Ambs-ace* is more fully anſwered. So his proof looks another way from his propoſition. His propoſition is, that *the caſting of* Ambs-ace *was neceſſary before it was thrown.* His proof is that it was neceſſary *when it was thrown*, examine all his cauſes over and over, and they will not afford him one grain of antecedent neceſſity. The firſt cauſe is in the *Dice*: True, if they be falſe Dice

there

there may be something in it, but then his contingency is destroyed. If they be square Dice, they have no more inclination to *Ambs-ace*, than to Cinque and Quater, or any other cast. His second cause is *the posture of the parties hand*: But what necessity was there that he should put his hand into such a posture. None at all. The third cause is *the measure of the force applied by the caster*. Now for the credit of his cause let him but name, I will not say a convincing reason, nor so much as a probable reason, but even any pretence of reason, how the Caster was necessitated from without himself to apply just so much force, and neither more or lesse. If he cannot, his cause is desperate, and he may hold his peace for ever, his last cause is *the posture of the Table*. But tell us in good earnest what necessity there was why the Caster must throw into that Table rather than the other, or that the Dice must fall just upon that part of the Table, *before the cast was thrown*: He that makes these to be necessary causes, I do not wonder if he make all effects necessary effects. If any one of these *causes* be contingent, it is sufficient to render the cast contingent, and now that they are all so contingent, yet he will needs have the effect to be necessary. And so it is when the cast is thrown, but not before the cast was thrown, which he undertook to prove: who can blame him for being so angry with the School-men, and their distinctions of necessity into absolute and hypothetical, seeing they touch his freehold so nearly.

But though his instance of raining to morrow be impertinent, as being no free action, yet because he triumphs so much in his argument, I will

not

not stick to go a little out of my way to meet a friend. For I confess, the validity of the reason had been the same, if he had made it of a free action, as thus: Either I shall finish this reply to morrow, or I shall not finish this reply to morrow, is a necessary proposition. But because he shall not complain of any disadvantage in the alteration of his terms; I will for once adventure upon his shower of rain. And first, I readily admit his major that this proposition (either it will rain to morrow, or it will not rain to morrow, is necessarily true, for of two contradictory propositions), the one must of necessity be true, because no third can be given. But his minor that *it could not be necessarily true, except one of the Members were necessarily true*, is most false. And so is his proof likewise. That *if neither the one nor the other of the Members be necessarily true, it cannot be affirmed that either the one, or the other is true*. A conjunct proposition may have both parts false, and yet the proposition be true, as if the Sun shine, it is day, is a true proposition at midnight. And T. H. confesseth as much, *Numb.* 19. *If I shall live I shall eat, is a necessary proposition, that is to say, it is necessary that that proposition should be true whensoever uttered. But it is not the necessity of the thing, nor is it therefore necessary that the man shall live, or that the man shall eat.* And so T. H. proceeds, *I do not use to fortifie my distinctions with such reasons.* But it seemeth he hath forgotten himself, and is contented with such poor fortifications. And though both parts of a disjunctive proposition cannot be false, because if it be a right disjunction, the Members are re-

pugnant,

pugnant, whereof one part is infallibly true, yet vary put the proposition a little to abate the edge of the disjunctions, and you shall finde that which *T. H.* saith to be true, that *it is not the necessity of the thing* which makes the proposition to be true. As for example vary it thus: *I know that either it will rain to morrow, or that it will not rain to morrow* is a true proposition: But it is not true that I know it will rain to morrow, neither is it true that I know it will not rain to morrow, wherefore the certain truth of the proposition doth not prove, that either of the Members is determinately true in present. Truth is a conformity of the understanding to the thing known, whereof speech is an interpreter. If the understanding agree not with the thing it is an errour, if the words agree not with the understanding it is a lie. Now the thing known is known either in it self, or in its causes. If it be known in it self, as it is, then we expresse our apprehension of it in words of the present tence, as *the Sun is risen*. If it be known in its cause, we expresse our selves in words of the future tense, as *to morrow will be an Eclipse of the Moon*. But if we neither know it in its self, nor in its causes, then there may be a foundation of truth, but there is no such determinate truth of it, that we can reduce it into a true proposition, we cannot say it doth rain to morrow, or it doth not rain to morrow. That were not onely false but absurd, we cannot positively say it will rain to morrow, because we do not know it in its causes, either how they are determined, or that they are determined, wherefore the certitude and evidence of

the

the disjunctive proposition is neither founded upon that which will be actually to morrow, for it is granted that we do not know that. Nor yet upon the determination of the causes, for then we would not say indifferently, either it will rain, or it will not rain, but positively it will rain, or positively it will not rain. But it is grounded upon an undeniable principle, that of two contradictory propositions, the one must necessarily be true. And therefore to say, either this, or that will infallibly be, but it is not yet determined whether this, or that shall be, is no such senseless assertion that it deserved a *Tytyrice Tupatulice*, but an evident truth which no man that hath his eyes in his head can doubt of.

If all this will not satisfie him, I will give one of his own kinde of proofs, that is an instance. That which necessitates all things according to *T. H.* is the decree of God, or that order which is set to all things by the eternal cause (*Numb. 11.*) Now God himself, who made this necessitating decree, was not subjected to it in the making thereof, neither was there any former order to oblige the first cause necessarily to make such a decree, therefore this decree being an act *ad extra* was freely made by God without any necessitation. Yet nevertheless, this disjunctive proposition is necessarily true. *Either God did make such a decree, or he did not make such a decree.* Again, though *T. H.* his opinion were true that all events are necessary, and that the whole Christian world are deceived, who believe that some events are free from necessity, yet he will not deny but if it ha been the good pleasure of God, he might

have

have made some causes free from necessity, seeing that it neither argues any imperfection, nor implies any contradiction. Supposing therefore that God had made some second causes free from any such antecedent determination to one, yet the former disjunction would be necessarily true. Either this free undetermined cause will act after this manner, or it will not act after this manner. Wherefore the necessary truth of such a disjunctive proposition doth not prove, that either of the members of the disjunction singly considered, is determinately true in present, but onely that the one of them will be determinately true to morrow.

T. H.

The last thing, in which also consisteth the whole controversy, Namely, that there is no such thing as an Agent, which when all things requisite to action are present, can nevertheless forbeare to produce it, or (which is all one) that there is no such thing as freedom from necessity, is easily inferd from that which hath been before alledged. For, if it be an Agent, it can work, And if it work, there is nothing wanting of what is requisite to produce the action, and consequently, the cause of the action is sufficient. And if sufficient, then also necessary, as hath been proved before.

J. D.

J. D.

I Wonder that *T. H.* should confess, that the whole weight of this controversy doth rest upon this proposition. *That there is no such thing as an Agent, which, when all things requisite to action are present, can nevertheless forbear to act*; And yet bring nothing but such poor Bull-rushes to support it. *If it be an Agent* (saith he) *it can work*, what of this? *A posse ad esse non valet argumentum*, from *can work*, to *will work*, is a weak inference. And from *will work*, to doth work upon absolute necessity, is another gross inconsequence. He proceeds thus, *If it work, there is nothing wanting of what is requisite to produce the action*, True, there wants nothing to produce that which is produced, but there may want much to produce that which was intended, One horse may pull his heart out, and yet not draw the Coach whither it should be, if he want the help or concurrence of his fellowes. *And consequently* (saith he) *the cause of the action is sufficient*. Yes sufficient to do what it doth, though perhaps with much prejudice to it self, but not alwayes sufficient to do what it should do, or what it would do. As he that begets a Monster should beget a man, and would beget a man, if he could. The last link of his argument follows; *And if sufficient, then also necessary*, stay there; by his leave there is no necessary connexion between sufficiency and efficiency,

ficiency, otherwise God himself should not be All-sufficient. Thus his Argument is vanished. But I will deal more favourably with him, and grant him all that, which he labours so much in vain to prove, That every effect in the world hath sufficient causes: Yea more, that supposing the determination of the free and contingent causes, every effect in the world is necessary. But all this will not advantage his cause the black of a bean, for still it amounts but to an hypotheticall necessity, and differs as much from that absolute necessity, which he maintains, as a Gentleman, who travailes for his pleasure, differs from a banished man, or a free Subject from a slave.

T. H.

Numb. 36. *AND thus you see how the inconveniences, which he objecteth must follow upon the holding of necessity, are avoided, and the necessity it self demonstratively prooved. To which I could add, if I thought it good Logick, the inconveniency of denying necessity, as that it distroyes both the Decrees and Prescience of God Almighty; for whatsoever God hath purposed to bring to pass by man as an instrument, or foreseeth shall come to passe, A man, if he have Liberty, such as he affirmeth from necessitation, might frustrate, and make not to come to pass. And God should either not foreknow it, and not Decree it, or he should foreknow such things shall be as shall never be, and decree that which shall never come to pass.*

J. D.

J. D.

THus he hath laboured in vain to satisfie my reasons, and to proove his own assertion. But for demonstration there is nothing like it among his Arguments. Now he saith, he could add other Arguments, if he thought it good Logick. There is no impediment in Logick, why a man may not press his Adversary with those absurdities which flow from his opinion, *Argumentum ducens ad impossibile*, or, *ad absurdum*, is a good form of reasoning. But there is another reason of his forbearance, though he be loth to express it.---- *Hæret lateri lathalis arundo*. The Arguments drawn from the attributes of God do stick so close in the sides of his cause, that he hath no mind to treate of that subject. By the way take notice of his own confession, that *he could add other reasons, if he thought it good Logick*. If it were predetermined in the outward causes, that he must make this very defence and no other, how could it be in his power to add or substract any thing. Just as if a blind-man should say in earnest, I could see, if I had mine eyes: Truth often breaks out, whilest men seek to smother it. But let us view his Argument: If a man have liberty from necessitation, he may frustrate the Decrees of God, and make his prescience false. First, for the Decrees of God, This is his Decree, that man should be a free Agent; If he did consider God, as a most simple Act without priority or posteriority of time, or any composition, He would not conceive of his Decrees, as of the Lawes of the *Medes* and *Persians*, long since enacted, and passed before we were born, but as coexistent with our selves, and with the acts which we do, by vertue of those Decrees. Decrees and Attributes are but notions to help the weaknefs of our understanding to conceive of God. The Decrees of God, are God himself, and therefore justly said to be before the foundation of the world was laid. And yet coexistent with our selves, because of the Infinite and Eternall being of God. The summe is this, The Decree of God, or God himself Eternally constitutes or ordaines all effects which come to to pass in time, according to the distinct natures or capacities of his creatures. An Eternal Ordination, is neither past nor to come, but alwaies present. So free actions do proceed, as well from the Eternall Decree of God as necessary, and from that order which he hath set in the world.

As the Decree of God is Eternall, so is his Knowledge. And therefore to speak truly and properly, there is neither fore-knowledge nor after-knowledge in him. The Knowledge of God comprehends all times in a point by reason of the eminence & vertue of its infinite perfection. And yet I confess, that this is called fore-knowledge, in respect of us. But this fore-knowledge doth produce no absolute necessity. Things are not therefore, because they are fore-known, but

therefore

therfore they are fore-known, becaufe they fhall come to pafs. If any thing fhould come to pafs otherwife than it doth, yet Gods knowledge could not be irritated by it, for then he did not know that it fhould come to pafs, as now it doth. Becaufe every knowledge of vifion neceffarily prefuppofeth its object. God did know, that *Judas* fhould betray Chrift; but *Judas* was not neceffitated to be a traitor by Gods knowledge. If *Judas* had not betrayed Chrift, then God had not fore-known that *Judas* fhould betray him. The cafe is this; A watch-man ftanding on the fteeples-top, as it is the ufe in *Germany*, gives notice to them below (who fee no fuch things) that company are coming, and how many; His prediction is moft certain, for he fees them. What a vain collection were it for one below to fay, what if they do not come, then a certaine prediction may fail. It may be urged, that there is a difference between thefe two cafes. In this cafe the coming is prefent to the Watch-man, but that which God fore-knowes is future. God knowes what fhall be; The Watch-man onely knowes what is. I anfwer, that this makes no difference at all in the cafe, by reafon of that difparity which is between Gods knowledge and ours: As that coming is prefent to the Watchman, which is future to them who are below: So all thofe things, which are future to us, are prefent to God, becaufe his Infinite and Eternall knowledge, doth reach to the future being of all Agents and events. Thus much is plainly acknowledged by *T. H.* Numb. 11. That *fore-knowledge is knowledge, and knowledge depends on the existence of the things known, and not they on it.* To conclude, the prescience of God doth not make things more necessary, than the production of the things themselves; But if the Agents were free Agents, the production of the things doth not make the events to be absolutely necessary, but onely upon supposition that the causes were so determined. Gods prescience prooveth a necessity of infallibility, but not of antecedent extrinsecall determination to one. If any event should not come to pass, God did never foreknow, that it would come to pass. For every knowledge necessarily presupposeth its object.

T. H.

Numb. 37. *This is all that hath come into my mind touching this question, since I last considered it. And I humbly beseech your Lordship to communicate it onely to* J. D. *And so praying God to prosper your Lordship in all your designes, I take leave, and am my most Noble and obliging Lord,*

Your most humble servant
T. H.

J. D.

J. D.

HE is very carefull to have this discourse kept secret, as appeares in this Section, and in the 14. and 15. Sections. If his answer had been kept private, I had saved the labour of a Reply. But hearing that it was communicated, I thought my self obliged to vindicate, both the truth and my self. I do not blame him to be cautious, for in truth, this assertion is of desperate consequence, and destructive to piety, policy, and morality. If he had desired to have kept it secret, the way had been to have kept it secret himself. It will not suffice to say as Numb. 14. that *Truth is Truth*; This the common plea of all men. Neither is it sufficient for him to say, as Numb. 15. That *it was desired by me*, long before that he had discovered his opinion by word of mouth. And my desire was to let some of my noble friends see the weakness of his grounds, and the pernicious consequences of that opinion. But if he think that this ventilation of the question between us two may do hurt, truly I hope not. The edge of his discourse is so abated, that it cannot easily hurt any rationall man, who is not too much possessed with prejudice.

T. H.

T. H.

Numb. 38. *POstscript, Arguments seldom work on men of wit and learning, when they have once ingaged themselves in a contrary opinion. If any thing do it, it is the shewing of them the causes of their errours, which is this; Pious men attribute to God Almighty for honour sake, whatsoever they see is honourable in the world, as seeing, hearing, willing, knowing, Justice, Wisedom, &c. But deny him such poor things as eyes, ears, brains, and other organs, without which, we wormes, neither have, nor can conceive such faculties to be; and so far they do well. But when they dispute of Gods actions Philosophically, then they consider them again, as if he had such faculties, and in that manner, as we have them, this is not well, and thence it is they fall into so many difficulties. We ought not to dispute of Gods Nature, he is no fit subject of our Philosophy. True Religion consisteth in obedience to Christ's Lieutenants, and in giving God such honour, both in attributes and actions, as they in their severall Lieutenancies shall ordain.*

J. D.

THough Sophisticall captions do seldom work on men of wit and learning, because by constant use they have their senses exercised to discern both good and evill, Heb. 5. 14. Yet solide
and

and substantiall reasons work sooner upon them than upon weaker judgments. The more exact the balance is, the sooner it discovers the reall weight, that is put into it. Especially if the proofs be proposed without passion or opposition. Let Sophisters and seditious Oratours apply themselves to the many headed multitude, because they despaire of success with *men of wit and learning*. Those whose gold is true, are not afraid to have it tryed by the touch. Since the former way hath not succeeded, *T. H.* hath another to shew, as the causes of our errours, which he hopes will proove more succesfull. When he sees he can do no good by fight, he seeks to circumvent us, under colour of curtesy, *Fistula dulce canit volucrem dum decipit auceps*. As they, who behold themselves in a glass, take the right hand for the left, and the left for the right, (*T. H.* knowes the comparison) so we take our own errours to be truths, and other mens truths to be errours. If we be in an errour in this, it is such an errour as we sucked from nature it self, such an errour as is confirmed in us by reason and experience, such an errour as God himself in his sacred Word hath revealed, such an errour as the Fathers and Doctors of the Church of all ages have delivered, Such an errour wherein we have the concurrence of all the best Philosophers, both Natural and Moral, such an errour as bringeth to God, the glory of Justice and Wisedom & Goodness, and Truth, such an errour as renders men more devout, more pious, more industrious

ous, more humble, more penitent for their sins. Would he have us resign up all these advantages to dance blindfold after his pipe. No, he perswades us too much to our loss. But let us see what is the imaginary cause of an imaginary errour. Forsooth, because we attribute to God whatsoever is honourable in the world, as seeing, hearing, willing, knowing, Justice Wisedom, but deny him such poor things, as eyes, ears, brains, and so far he saith we do well. He hath reason, for since we are not able to conceive of God as he is, the readiest way we have, is by remooving all that imperfection from God, which is in the creatures. So we call him Infinite, Immortall, Independent. Or by attribubuting to him all those perfections, which are in the creatures after a most eminent manner, so we call him Best, Greatest, most Wise, most Just, most Holy. But saith he, *When they dispute of Gods actions Philosophically, then they consider them again, as if he had such faculties, and in the manner as we have them.*

And is this the cause of our errour? That were strange indeed, for they who dispute Philosophically of God, do neither ascribe faculties to to him in that manner that we have them, Nor yet do they attribute any proper faculties at all to God. Gods Understanding, and his Will is his very Essence, which for the eminency of its infinite perfection, doth perform all those things alone, in a most transcendent manner, which reasonable creatures do perform imperfectly,

by

by distinct faculties. Thus to dispute of God with modesty, and reverence, and to clear the Deity from the imputation of tyranny, injustice, and dissimulation, which none do throw upon God with more presumption, than those who are the Patrons of absolute necessity, is both comely and Christian.

It is not the desire to discover the originall of a supposed errour, which drawes them ordinarily into these exclamations, against those who dispute of the Deity. For some of themselves dare anatomise God, and publish his Eternall Decrees with as much confidence, as if they had been all their lives of his cabinet councell. But it is for fear, lest those pernicious consequences, which flow from that doctrine essentially, and reflect in so high a degree upon the supreme goodness, should be laid open to the view of the world; Just as the Turks do, first establish a false religion of their own devising, and then forbid all men upon pain of death to dispute upon religion; Or as the Priests of *Molech* (the Abhomination of the Ammonites) did, make a noise with their timbrells all the while the poor Infants were passing through the fire in *Tophet*, to keep their pitifull cries from the eares of their Parents: So they make a noise with their declamations against those, who dare dispute of the nature of God, that is, who dare set forth his Justice, and his goodness, and his truth, and his Philanthropy, onely to deaf the ears, and dim the eyes of the Christian world,

least

(252)

least they should hear the lamentable ejulations and howlings, or see, that ruefull spectacle of millions of souls tormented for evermore in the flames of the true *Tophet*, that is Hell, onely for that which according to *T. H.* his doctrine was never in their power to shun, but which they were ordered and inevitably necessitated to do. Onely to expresss the omnipotence and dominion, and to satisfie the pleasure of him, who is in truth the *Father of all mercies, and the God of all consolation*. This is life eternall (saith our Saviour) to know the *onely true God* and *Jesus Christ*, whom he hath sent. Joh. 17. 3. *Pure Religion and undefiled before God, and the Father, is this, to visite the fatherless and widowes in their affliction, and to keep himself unspotted from the world*, saith St. *James*, Jam. 1. 27. *Fear God and keep his Commandements, for this is the whole duty of man*, saith *Salomon*, *Eccles.* 12. 13. But *T.H.* hath found out a more compendious way to heaven: *True Religion* (faith he) *consisteth in obedience to Christs Lieutenants, and giving God such honour both in attributes and actions, as they in their severall Lieutenances shall ordain*. That is to say, be of the Religion of every Christian Country where you come. To make the Civill Magistrate to be Christs Lieutenant upon earth, for matters of Religion; And to make him to be Supreme Judge in all controversies, whom all must obey, is a doctrine so strange, and such an uncouth phrase to Christian eares, that I should have

have missed his meaning, but that I consulted with his Book, *De Cive* c. 15. Sect. 16. and c. 17. Sect. 28. What if the Magistrate shall be no Christian himself? What if he shall command contrary to the Law of God, or Nature, *Must we obey him rather than God?* Act. 14. 19. Is the Civill Magistrate become now the onely *ground and pillar of Truth?* I demand then why *T. H.* is of a different mind from his soveraign, and from the Lawes of the Land concerning the attributes of God and his Decrees? This is a new Paradox, and concerns not this question of liberty, and necessity? Wherefore I forbear to prosecute it further, and so conclude my reply with the words of the Christian Poet,

> *Cæsaris jussum est ore Galieni*
> *Princeps quod colit ut colemus omnes,*
> *Æternum colemus Principem dierum,*
> *Factorem Dominumq; Galieni.*

FINIS.